FTCE Exceptional Student Education (ESE) - 2nd Edition

By: Kathleen Jasper, Ed.D. & Jeremy M. Jasper, M.Ed.

August 2019

NAVAED

NavaED
10600 Chevrolet Way #107
Estero, FL 33928

FTCE - Exceptional Student Education (ESE) - 2nd Edition

Printed in the United States of America

ISBN: 9781086619805

The competencies in this book were designed and implemented by the Florida Department of Education. Visit www.fl.nesinc.com for more information.

Table of Contents

NAVAED

Test Information

Exceptional Student Education (ESE) K-12

Testing time is 2 hours and 30 minutes

Approximately 120 questions (1 minute and 15 seconds per questions)

Maximum percent of correct questions needed to achieve a scale score of 200-70% (As of 12/2018)

Approximately 84 out of 120 questions needed to pass

About this Study Guide

This study guide is designed using the state standards, competencies, and specifications set by the state of Florida for exceptional student education in kindergarten through twelfth grade. The information represents a broad overview of skills and knowledge that are necessary to be successful on the exam.

It is important to remember that as you prepare for this exam, don't rely heavily on your own personal experiences. This test is designed to showcase a perfect world scenario in exceptional student education (ESE). Keeping with this theme, the following overarching ideals will be key in managing the correct perspective for this test:

- You have every possible resource available to you. Answer the questions as if you have all the money, time, ability, paraprofessionals, availability, technology, etc. This will help by not setting limits on how you answer the questions as if you were in your own classroom and the challenges that come with it.
- Student achievement at a high level of critical thinking is paramount, no matter what type of student, especially exceptional students. Whether it is questioning techniques, assignments, assessments, or any other engagement with the student, the importance is comprehension and critical thinking.
- You are differentiating and accommodating every minute of the teaching day. In the real world, this may not be entirely achievable, but don't limit yourself as you choose the correct answers based on how it is in the real world.
- Technology is key. There is an emphasis on technology in the classroom. Therefore, when determining which answer choice is the best one, choose the that emphasizes students' use of technology.
- Florida is a multicultural state, therefore multiculturalism in the classroom must be addressed. Answer choices that incorporate multicultural strategies, techniques, and content should have priority.
- As a teacher (in this test) you are keeping data folders and portfolios on every single one of your students. You are using these tools to progress monitor at all times that way instruction is tailored to each individual student to allow for successful academic achievement.
- Anything pertaining to the state standards is always the correct answer. The state administers this exam. The state standards are the main pillar of the exam.
- Everything you do is for the success of the student, no matter what.
- Have inclusive mindset. ESE students have every right to be treated and accepted like everyone else. ESE students should also be actively participating in all classroom activities, especially the challenging tasks. Everyone has something to contribute.

Competency 1
Knowledge of Foundations of Exceptional Student Education

1. Identify state and federal legislation that govern the education of students with exceptionalities.
2. Classify the characteristics of students with exceptionalities using the eligibility criteria of categories included in current state and federal laws and regulations governing K–12 educational programs.
3. Compare typical and atypical development of physical, cognitive, linguistic, social, and emotional stages of students in the K–12 educational system.
4. Interpret principles and practices in the provision of education for students with exceptionalities based on legal and ethical standards.
5. Apply knowledge of the requirements for developing individual educational plans (IEPs), educational plans (EPs), and transition IEPs.
6. Evaluate the role and function of systemwide models of support for assisting all students, including students with exceptionalities, in accessing the general education curriculum and achieving high expectations.
7. Apply effective methods of communication, consultation, and collaboration with students, parents, caregivers, and all other stakeholders, including those from culturally and linguistically diverse backgrounds, as equal members of educational teams.
8. Use effective methods for coaching and supporting paraprofessionals, tutors, and volunteers to assist students with exceptionalities across settings.
9. Determine the purposes and functions of professionals, advocacy organizations, and agencies relevant to educating students with exceptionalities.
10. Determine the factors associated with disproportionality in exceptional student education.

Competency 1 makes up 24% of the exam or approximately 29 questions.

Federal Regulation – Exceptional Student Education

IDEA 2004 Individuals with Disabilities Education Act 2004 (IDEA). IDEA is a law that makes available a free appropriate public education to eligible children with disabilities throughout the nation and ensures special education and related services to those children.

The IDEA governs how states and public agencies provide early intervention, special education, and related services to more than 6.5 million eligible infants, toddlers, children, and youth with disabilities (U.S. Department of Education, 2019).

Remember

Children and youth ages 3 through 21 receive special education and related services under IDEA Part B.

Family Educational Rights and Privacy Act (FERPA). FERPA is a Federal law that protects the privacy of student education records. The law applies to all schools that receive funds under an applicable program of the U.S. Department of Education.

FERPA gives parents certain rights with respect to their children's education records. These rights transfer to the student when he or she reaches the age of 18 or attends a school beyond the high school level (U.S. Department of Education, 2019).

Every Student Succeeds Act (ESSA).

Advances equity by upholding critical protections for America's disadvantaged and high-need students. Requires all students in America be taught to high academic standards that will prepare them to succeed in college and careers. Ensures that vital information is provided to educators, families, students, and communities through annual statewide assessments that measure students' progress toward those high standards (U.S. Department of Education, 2019).

> **Quick Tip!**
>
> Every student receiving ESE services has the right to a **free appropriate public education (FAPE).** This means that the local public-school district must provide services designed to help students meet their annual goals and make progress in the general curriculum at no cost to the parent (Florida Department of Education, 2012).

No Child Left Behind 2002 (NCLB). NCLB introduced accountability to public schools.

Title I: Improving academic achievement of the disadvantaged

Title II: Preparing, training, and recruiting high quality teachers and principals

Title III: language instruction for limited English proficient and immigrant students

Title IV: 21st Century Schools

Title V: Promoting informed parental choice and innovative programs

Title VI: Flexibility and accountability

Race to the Top (RTTT)*.* Forty-six states and the District of Columbia submitted comprehensive reform plans to compete in the Race to the Top competition. While 19 states have received funding so far, 34 states modified state education laws or policies to facilitate needed change, and 48 states worked together to create a voluntary set of rigorous college- and career-ready standards (The White House, 2018).

The Consent Decree. Grounded in the 14th Amendment and the result of League of United Latin American Citizens (LULAC) vs. State Board of Education, the Consent Decree protects English Language Learners (ELL) and their right to a free, comprehensible education. It addresses civil and academic rights of ELL students and requires instruction be delivered in a comprehensible manner so ELLs can fully participate. Since 1975, federal law has required that students with disabilities have access to school and a free appropriate public education.

Section 504 of the Rehabilitation Act of 1973. Section 504 regulations require a school district to provide a "free appropriate public education" (FAPE) to each qualified student with a disability who is in the school district's jurisdiction, regardless of the nature or severity of the disability. Under Section 504, FAPE consists of the provision of regular or special education and related aids and services designed to meet the student's individual educational needs as adequately as the needs of nondisabled students are met (U.S. Department of Education, 2015).

> **Keep in mind!**
>
> In some cases, students are English Language Learners (ELL) and in Exceptional Student Education (ESE). Therefore, IDEA and the Consent Decree are two federal regulations to keep in mind when providing education to these students.

Americans with Disabilities Act of 1990 (ADA). ADA is a civil rights law that prohibits discrimination based on disability. It provides similar protections against discrimination to Americans with disabilities as the Civil Rights Act of 1964 (U.S. Department of Education, 2015).

Exceptional Student Education Categories

According to the Florida Department of Education (2011), the Bureau of Exceptional Education and Student Services supports school districts and others in their efforts to provide ESE programs for students ages 3–21 who have disabilities and students who are gifted. Each school district is responsible for providing services to students who are eligible.

Exceptionality	Description
(ASD) Autism spectrum disorder	Developmental disability affecting verbal/nonverbal communication and social interaction which tends to have an impact on educational performance. Characteristics associated with autism include: • Engaging in repetitive activities and stereotyped movements • Resistance to environmental change or change in daily routines • Unusual responses to sensory experiences • **Echolalia-**repetition and echoing of words and sounds
(DHH) Deaf or hard-of-hearing	Impairment so severe that it impedes the processing of linguistic information through hearing with or without amplification. This has adverse effects on a child's educational performance.
(DD) Developmentally Delayed	A student who is developmentally delayed has a deficit in one or more of the following areas: • Adaptive or self-help development • Cognitive development • Communication development • Social/emotional development • Physical/motor development
(DSI) Dual-sensory impaired (deaf-blind)	Simultaneous hearing and visual impairments which cause severe communication, acquisition of information, and functionality within the environment deficits.
(EBD) Emotional or behavioral disabilities	One or more of the following characteristics over a period of time to the extent that it adversely affects educational performance: • Inability to learn that cannot be explained by intellectual, sensory, or health factors • Inability to maintain adequate interpersonal relationships with peers and teachers • Inappropriate types of behavior or feelings under normal circumstances • A general prevalent mood of unhappiness or depression • Tendency to develop physical symptoms or fears associated with personal or academic issues
(HH) Homebound or hospitalized	Restriction of activities over an extended period of time based upon a medically diagnosed or psychiatric condition either acute or catastrophic in nature. This also includes chronic illness or repeated intermittent illness that confines the student to home or hospital.

(InD) Intellectual disabilities	Significant subaverage general intellectual functioning and deficits in adaptive behavior manifested during birth through 18 years of age.
(OHI) Other health impairment	Having limited strength, vitality, or alertness, including a heightened alertness to environmental stimuli, that results in limited alertness to the educational environment and due to chronic or acute health problems. These may include: • Asthma • Attention Deficit Disorder (ADD) • Attention Deficit Hyperactivity Disorder (ADHD) • Diabetes • Epilepsy • Heart condition • Hemophilia • Lead poisoning • Leukemia • Nephritis • Rheumatic fever • Tourette syndrome • Sickle cell anemia **Quick Tip!** Students with Attention Deficit and Hyperactivity Disorder (ADHD) fall under ***other health impairment*** (OHI). While some may think that ADHD is a behavioral disorder, it is not classified as a behavior disorder.
(OI) Orthopedic impairment	Severe skeletal, muscular, or neuromuscular impairments resulting from congenital anomalies and impairments from other causes. These include skeletal deformity, spina bifida, cerebral palsy, or amputations.
(TBI) Traumatic brain injury	Injury to the brain caused by an external force resulting in total or partial functional disability, psychosocial impairment, or both. Applies to open or closed head injuries with impairments in one or more of the following areas of cognition, language, memory, attention, reasoning, abstract thinking, judgment, problem-solving, sensory, perceptual, and motor abilities, psychosocial behavior, physical functions, information processing, and speech.
(SLD) Specific learning disabilities	Disorder in one or more of the basic psychological processes involved in understanding or in using spoken or written language that may develop into the imperfect ability to listen, think, speak, read, write, spell, or do mathematical calculations. Conditions included are perceptual disabilities, brain injury, minimal brain dysfunction, dyslexia, and developmental aphasia. This does NOT include learning problems that are the result of visual, motor, or hearing disabilities, intellectual disability, emotional disturbance, or environmental, cultural, or economic disadvantage.
(SI) Speech impairment	Disorders of speech sounds, fluency, or voice that interfere with communication which may include stuttering, impaired articulation, or voice impairment.
(LI) Language impairment	Disorders of language that interfere with communication and one or more of the basic learning processes (phonology, morphology, syntax, semantics, and pragmatics) involved in spoken or written language.
(VI) Visually impaired	Includes students who are blind, have no vision, low vision, visual impairment after best correction, students diagnosed with a progressive condition that will result in visual impairment or no vision after best correction.

Developmental Stages

Children go through developmental stages as they grow. It is important that ESE teachers know these stages, so they can spot typical and atypical cognitive, physical, and emotional development in children.

Piaget – Stages of Cognitive Development

Perhaps the most widely used framework when analyzing child development is Piaget's stages of cognitive development. Piaget asserted that cognitive development was a reorganization of mental processes resulting from biological maturation and environmental experience (1972).

Piaget's 4 Stages of Cognitive Development		
Sensorimotor	0–2 years	Children at this stage figure out the world through sensory and motor experiences. Object permanence and separation anxiety are hallmarks of this stage.
Pre-operational	2–6 years	Children at this stage identify and use symbols for objects but do not have the ability to apply logical reasoning. They know how to play pretend and are egocentric.
Concrete operational	7–12 years	Logical reasoning about concrete objects kicks in during this stage. Conservation, reversibility, serial ordering, and understanding cause and effect relationships are hallmarks of this stage, but thinking is still limited to the concrete.
Formal operational	12 years–adult	Abstract thinking such as logic, deductive reasoning, comparison, and classification are demonstrated by the individual in this stage.

(Piaget, 1972)

Atypical Child Development. Atypical development means a child does not develop normally. This can result in developmental disabilities. Developmental disabilities are a group of conditions due to a physical, neurological, learning, language, or behavior impairment. These conditions impact day-to-day functioning and usually last throughout a person's lifetime (Rubin and Crocker, 1989).

Educating ESE Students Based on Legal and Ethical Standards

According to the Florida Department of Education (2012), laws governing ESE are organized around the following 6 principles:

1. **Parent and Student Participation**

   Parents should have a voice in ***ALL*** discussions and decisions about their child's education. As students get older, their own ***participation*** becomes important. In fact, once students are 14 years old, they are included in ESE meetings to help make decisions about their education. *See self-determination in competency 6.*

2. **Appropriate Evaluation**

   A team of people conduct an individual evaluation *on* a student's educational strengths and needs. The evaluation includes data collection regarding instruction and interventions over time. This includes interviews, observations, and analyses of all information available. The evaluation sometimes includes individual tests given by a specialist, such as a psychologist or speech-language pathologist. The law requires ESE students to be reevaluated to measure student progress and implement changes as needed.

3. **Individual Educational Plan (IEP)**

   An ***IEP*** is a written agreement outlining services the school will provide to help the ESE student meet his or her educational needs.

6 steps in the process of planning and delivering ESE services:

1. Evaluation
2. Eligibility determination
3. Developing the first individual educational plan
4. Consent for services
5. Annual reviews
6. Reevaluations

4. **Free Appropriate Public Education (FAPE)**

   Every student receiving ESE services has the right to a free appropriate public education. This means that the local public-school district must provide services designed for ESE students to meet their annual goals and make progress in the general curriculum at no cost to the parent.

   Students who live in Florida, who are at least three years old and less than 22 years old, who meet the eligibility criteria, and who have not yet graduated from high school with a standard diploma, are entitled to receive free exceptional education services from the local public-school district.

5. **Least Restrictive Environment (LRE)**

   Children with disabilities have the right to receive their education in the school and the classroom they would attend if they were not disabled. However, some students need special classes or services. Only then should they be removed from the general classroom. The goal is to keep ESE students included in the general curriculum.

6. **Procedural Safeguards**

   School and district staff must follow certain steps to make sure exceptional student education and related services meet the unique needs of each public-school student with a disability.

(Florida Department of Education, 2012)

Individual Education Plan (IEP)

If the child is eligible for exceptional student education (ESE) services, the next step is to hold a meeting to write an IEP.

IEP Meeting Notification

Parents/guardians of ESE students must be notified of the IEP meeting 2 weeks prior to the meeting. Parents/guardians are notified via

IEP Team:

The IEP team decides which special services and supports the child needs to make progress and achieve his or her annual goals. The individuals that make up the team, as well as those who have the student's best educational interests in mind, are referred to as **stakeholders.** The IEP team includes:

- The parents of the child
- At least one teacher general education teacher
- At least one special education provider of the child
- Social personnel (psychologist, speech pathologist)
- Guidance counselor
- Other individuals who have knowledge or special expertise regarding the child
- The child (The child is part of the team and should be part of making IEP decisions.)

The IEP team also decides where the child will receive services. Most children with disabilities spend the majority of their school day in general education classrooms. Some children leave the general education classroom for part of the day to receive services in an ESE classroom. A small number of children spend all day in a special classroom or in a special school.

Goals

The IEP includes goals that the student and the IEP team create together. Throughout the year, teachers and the IEP team work with the student to help him or her achieve long-term and short-term goals. Goals should be created using the SMART method.

SMART stands for **S**pecific, **M**easurable, **A**chievable, **R**elevant, and **T**imely.

- **Specific** – states what the student will accomplish in very specific and detailed terms.
- **Measurable** – provides a way to evaluate student progress—using assessment data.
- **Achievable** – must be within the scope of abilities for the student.
- **Relevant** – must pertain to the student's current grade level, coursework, and abilities.
- **Timely** – must be completed within a targeted time frame.

SMART Goal Example:

Within the school year, Patricia will increase written language skills by using proper spelling and punctuation in 4 out of 5 trials with 80% accuracy as measured by informal assessments.

Accommodations

It is important to understand that teachers never make the curriculum easier or lower standards for ESE students. Instead, teachers provide support in the form of accommodations. These accommodations are listed on the IEP.

ESE accommodations can include:

- Assistive technology
- Environmental adaptations
  - Extra time for tests
  - Quiet area to perform tasks
- Specialized instructional strategies
- Peer support
- Curricular adaptations or modifications
- Collaborative teaching

> ***A Special Note on Technology***
>
> When taking the FTCE ESE, be sure to match the technology accommodation to the exceptionality. For example, a student who is visually impaired would need a screen reader for computer work.

Review and Revision of the IEP

IEP reviews must happen at least every 12 months. The IEP team decides how a child's progress will be measured and reported. The IEP team meets to talk about the child's progress and to develop a new IEP. The IEP team generally makes changes to the IEP at an IEP team meeting. Whenever changes are made to the IEP, the changes agreed to are documented in writing. Parents may request a copy of the revised IEP.

Transition IEP

The transition IEP is used for a student age 16 and older. The purpose of the transition IEP is to help the student transition into life after graduation from high school. This will be discussed further in detail during Competency 6.

Reevaluation IEP

The school must reevaluate ESE students every 3 years. During this reevaluation, the IEP team determines if a student should continue receiving ESE services or if the student should be dismissed from the ESE program.

Waivers for Students with Disabilities

Students with disabilities who entered grade 9 in 2014–15 and beyond are required to work toward a standard high school diploma and are expected to participate in statewide, standardized assessments. State law, however, provides for a waiver of statewide, standardized assessment graduation requirements for students with disabilities whose abilities cannot be accurately measured by the assessments. Pursuant to S. 1008.22(3)(c)2., F.S., "A student with a disability, as defined in s. 1007.02(2), for whom the IEP team determines that the statewide, standardized assessments under this section cannot accurately measure the student's abilities, taking into consideration all allowable accommodations, shall have assessment results waived for the purpose of receiving a course grade and a standard high school diploma. Such waiver shall be designated on the student's transcript."

External Support

Prior to instructional delivery, support materials are prepared. These may include accommodations, supplementary aids, and services and supports. The need for these materials is identified through collaborative planning between the general education teacher and ESE personnel. The IEP ultimately serves as the reference for all supports necessary.

In-Class Support

- **Co-Teacher**: a formal commitment between a general education teacher and an ESE teacher to jointly plan, deliver, and assess instructions for all student's in a general education classroom.
- **Support Facilitator**: an individual who provides a variety of supports to students and/or to the general education teacher that meets the needs identified through collaborative planning. This may include paraprofessionals, occupational therapists, physical therapists, speech, etc.
- **Peers:** students in the general education classroom are matched with ESE students to assist with classroom, physical, and social needs and may also provide instructional tutoring. Students would be paired for cooperative learning, group projects, or activities.

  ***NOTE:** Students should never be assigned to an ESE student in the same class as an aide or assistant; that is what a paraprofessional is for. The IEP will clearly state that a professional or trained personnel is to provide all services to students. *

Specialized Support

Provides focused services to students who require support to address one or more objectives in a setting other than the general education classroom for a period of time during the school day. This support is the result of an individual analysis of student needs and not on the basis of labels or settings such as content mastery, resource, or self-contained (Florida Professional Development Alternatives, 2016).

Least Restrictive Environment (LRE)

Students with disabilities will only be removed from a regular classroom if the nature or severity of their disability interferes to such a degree that education, even with additional supports and services, cannot be satisfactorily achieved in a regular class. Students must be placed in the least restrictive environment possible (Florida Department of Education, 2012).

Keeping ESE students in general classrooms helps to maintain equality. For example, a student with a disability should have the same opportunity to thrive in a regular classroom like any other student. It is only when the disability cannot be adequately accommodated for in the general classroom should the student be placed in a separate classroom. Providing students education in the least restrictive environment is essential.

Though the regular classroom is the first placement option for special education services to be considered, federal regulations and state laws also recognize that additional placement options may be necessary (Florida Department of Education 2012).

Florida Statute states that "[a] continuum of alternative exceptional education placements shall be available." (Section 230.22(2)(1)F.S.). This portion of the law is designed to ensure that each student is educated in the LRE that is appropriate for the student. **Among the specific options within the continuum are supplementary consultation, resource room, special class, self-contained class, special day school, or hospital/homebound instruction** (Section 230.22(2)(4)F.S.).

INCLUSION: ESE students should be in general education classrooms with all students.

Providing to all students, including those with significant disabilities, equitable opportunities to receive effective educational services, with the needed supplementary aids and support services, in age appropriate classrooms in their neighborhood schools, in order to prepare students for productive lives as full members of society.

National Center on Educational Restructuring and Inclusion (NCERI).

Individuals with Disabilities Education Improvement Act (IDEA 2004) continues to require school districts to educate children in the **least restrictive environment (LRE)**. Florida Statutes (F.S.) offer parallel language stating that "Special classes, separate schooling, or other removal of exceptional education students from regular classes shall occur only when the nature or severity of the handicap cannot be satisfactorily accommodated with supplementary aids and services in the regular classroom." (Section 230.22(2)(2) F.S.)

When discussing the least restrictive environment a student will receive free and appropriate education, the student's needs must be considered. A one size fits all approach cannot be used, therefore LRE decisions **cannot** be based on:

- The student's exceptionality
- Limited space in a program
- Administrative convenience
- Configuration of the school delivery system
- Cost or funding issues

Quick Tip!

Sometimes ESE students thrive in general, honors and even AP classes. Those students often receive **consult services** in the areas of speech or hearing. In these cases, students still have a disability, but the disability does not hinder their ability to achieve in the classroom. These students receive consultations periodically throughout the year as needed. This type of consultation is used to monitor grades and make sure the students are on track.

Parent Communication

Parents must be notified of the IEP meeting 2 weeks before the meeting. Parents receive invite via mail.

Teachers can (and should) communicate with parents/guardians as frequently as possible with positive behaviors, especially if they are replacing some not-so-desirable behaviors. While emails can be acceptable, phone calls are more personal. The main thing to communicate is that you want to work WITH the parent/guardian to help the student.

All communication with parents must be made in their native language. In the event a teacher does not speak the native language, a translator must be used to communicate effectively with the parent.

> ***Student-Centered Scenario***
>
> Kyle is a 6th grade student who is academically capable of completing grade-level assignments but often neglects to do so. While communication with the parents seems to be in order, the problem can actually be dealt with more directly by creating an academic contract between Kyle and his teachers.

Student Communication

Communicating with all stakeholders is essential, and this includes the students. Academic and behavioral expectations must be clearly communicated to achieve a positive learning environment for all students. This can include, but is not limited to:

- Setting clear classroom guidelines, rules, and expectations
- Providing a hard copy of the course outline to each student (secondary)
- Using nonverbal cues such as hand and eye gestures
- Providing a hard copy of a rubric to every student prior to a writing-based or project

Paraprofessionals

Special education paraprofessionals assist students who have special needs. Paraprofessionals work under the direction of a certified teacher. Paraprofessionals generally work in an inclusionary setting (i.e. least restrictive environment). The special education paraprofessional assists the general education teacher in a variety of ways. Paraprofessionals help instruct daily classroom activities and help special needs students. Paraprofessionals also care for students' physical and emotional health, while also ensuring a safe environment for the ESE student. Paraprofessionals affirm students' abilities and strive to promote dignity in all relationships. The paraprofessionals duties are dictated by the certified instructor in the room and they are not to stray from the objectives given. Instructors should conference with their paraprofessionals often and foster a good working relationship.

Professional Organizations Governing ESE

The National Association of Special Education Teachers (NASET) is a national membership organization dedicated to rendering all possible support and assistance to those preparing for or teaching in the field of special education. **NASET** was founded to promote the profession of special education teachers and to provide a national forum for their ideas.

The Council for Exceptional Children (CEC) advocates on behalf of children with exceptionalities. The CEC examines policy issues, develops appropriate responses to those issues and influences local, state, provincial and federal legislation.

The Division on Career Development and Transition of the Council for Exceptional Children promotes national and international efforts to improve the quality of, and access to, career/vocational and transition services, increase the participation of education in career development and transition goals, and to influence policies affecting career development and transition services for persons with disabilities.

Disproportionality in ESE

Too often, students who are struggling with reading or behavior will be labeled as disabled. However, they may just be struggling for a limited time. Mislabeling students as disabled leads to an overrepresentation of students in ESE. Often, students who are English Language Learners (ELL) will be labeled as ESE, when they do not have a learning disability, but rather are struggling with the language. Misidentified students are likely to encounter limited access to a rigorous curriculum and diminished expectations. More importantly, mislabeling students creates a false impression of the child's intelligence and academic potential. This is important for several reasons.

- Once students are receiving special education services, they tend to remain in special education classes (Harry & Klingner, 2006).
- Students are likely to encounter a limited, less rigorous curriculum (Harry & Klingner, 2006).
- Lower expectations can lead to diminished academic and post-secondary opportunities (National Research Council, 2002; Harry & Klingner, 2006).
- Students in special education programs can have less access to academically able peers (Donovan & Cross, 2002).
- Disabled students are often stigmatized socially (National Research Council, 2002).
- Disproportionality can contribute to significant racial separation (Harry & Klingner, 2006; Losen & Orfield, 2002).

Competency 2
Knowledge of Assessment and Evaluation

1. Determine the purposes and characteristics of different types of assessments and the appropriate use.
2. Apply the legal requirements and ethical principles regarding assessment of students with exceptionalities.
3. Identify measurement concepts (e.g., reliability and validity), characteristics, and uses of norm-referenced and criterion-referenced assessments for students with exceptionalities.
4. Determine the purpose and requirements for participation of students with disabilities in the statewide assessment program and available accommodations, waivers, and exemptions.
5. Interpret and apply the results of formal, informal, and performance-based assessments to address specific needs of students with exceptionalities.
6. Analyze assessment data to identify student needs and evaluate student progress in acquiring, generalizing, and maintaining skills across settings.

Competency 2 makes up 13% of the exam or approximately 16 questions

Assessment Types

Assessment Type	Definition	Example
Diagnostic	A pre-assessment providing instructors with information about students' prior knowledge, **preconceptions,** and **misconceptions** before beginning a learning activity.	Before starting a unit on earth space science, a teacher gives a quick assessment to determine students' knowledge, perceptions, and misconceptions about earth space science.
Formative	A range of formal and informal assessments or checks conducted by the teacher before, during, and after the learning process in order to modify instruction.	A teacher walks around the room checking on students as they read. She might also write anecdotal notes to review later to help her design further instruction.
Summative	An assessment that focuses on the outcome of a program or lesson. Summative assessments are often used to measure growth.	midterms, finals, final grades.
Criterion-Referenced	An assessment that measures student performance against a fixed set of predetermined criteria or learning standards.	The FCAT, EOC, and FSA are criterion-referenced tests.
Norm-Referenced (Percentile)	An assessment or evaluation that yields an estimate of the position of the tested individual in a predefined population with respect to the trait being measured.	The NAEP is an exam given every few years for data purposes only to compare students' reading scores across the U.S.

Authentic Assessment of Student Progress

Assessing student progress is an important component of teaching. Teachers can use an infinite number of strategies to monitor and assess student achievement.

Informal assessments, sometimes referred to as **formative** assessments and **alternative** assessments, are a great way to understand student progress. With informal assessments, teachers can target students' specific problem areas, adapt instruction, and intervene earlier rather than later.

Types of Authentic Assessments

> ***Quick Tip:*** Teachers often use oral assessments when working with English language learners (ELL). It is easier for students who speak another language to communicate through an oral assessment.

- ***Oral Assessments.*** Assessments that are conducted, either wholly or in part, by word of mouth. Oral assessments include:
  - Answering questions orally
  - Performances
  - Presentations
  - Role-play
- ***Written Assessments.*** Assessments where students write to communicate their learning. Written assessments often yield more information than a multiple-choice test. Teachers should use rubrics to assess written assessments. Written assessments include:
  - Essays
  - Lab write-up
  - Letters
  - Journals
- ***Performance-Based.*** Assessments where students are required to solve problems demonstrating their knowledge and skills. Performances-based assessments require students to perform a task rather than simply fill in multiple choice bubbles. Performance-based assessments are considered **authentic assessments** and include:
  - Participating in a lab or experiment
  - Solving and showing work for math problems
  - Engaging in role-play
  - Conducting a presentation
  - Building picture books

- ***Portfolios.*** Assessments where the teacher uses a series of student-developed artifacts to determine student learning. Portfolios are considered a form of **authentic** assessment and **alternative** assessment. Portfolios offer an **alternative** or an addition to traditional methods of grading and high-stakes exams. Portfolios are tools to help students establish short-term and long-term goals.

- **Progress monitoring** should be a component of student learning and assessment. Progress monitoring is when the teacher and the student track progress and modify instruction and behaviors to increase student learning. Students and teachers can progress monitor through a variety of ways including:
  - Data folders
  - Fluency checks
  - Portfolio
  - Conferences

Scenario: Mr. Rodriguez is sitting down with a 3rd grade student as they look over the work the student has completed over the last quarter. Mr. Rodriguez and his student then discuss short-term and long-term goals and a plan to reach those goals based on the data. They are progress monitoring using a portfolio review/assessment.

Behavior Managements in Assessments

Technique	Definition	Example
Shaping	Rewarding a child as she successfully improves the acquisition of a target skill. This is a slow manipulation of behavior.	Mr. Jones used shaping to help Julia learn to feed herself independently. He did this by helping Julia use the spoon hand over hand, moving to touching Julia's wrist until Julia was finally able to pick up her spoon and eat from her bowl independently.
Fading	Decreasing the level of assistance needed to complete a task or activity.	After he sees that Julia is beginning to feed herself, he decreases the number of times he helps her. Julia struggles a bit, but ultimately does the task herself.
Probing	When a student does not respond to a teacher question. The teacher can then probe or assist that support the student to answer.	Mr. Hernandez asks a student a question. The student responds incorrectly. Rather than saying, "That is incorrect." The teacher drops little hints and the student is able to figure it out.
Modeling	When students learn by observing the teacher. The teacher demonstrates a process, and the students watch.	Ms. Benson reads aloud from the text as students following along. She stops to sound out confusing words so students can see her process of working through the text.

State Assessments for ESE Students

Federal and state laws require that all students be included in statewide testing. Most students with disabilities take the state assessment in Florida along with general education students.

Examples of testing accommodations:

- A student is given extra time as suggested in her IEP.
- An interpreter uses sign language to give the directions for a test to a child who cannot hear.
- A student takes a three-hour test in three separate, one-hour sessions rather than in one long session.
- A student responds to the test questions orally rather than the way other students do, such as with paper and pencil or on a computer.

Testing Accommodations

Accommodations are changes or adjustments to standard testing procedures or materials that enable a student with a disability to participate in state or district assessments. Accommodations that negate the validity of a statewide standardized assessment are not allowable. The use of allowable accommodations is based on current instructional accommodations and the accessible materials used regularly by the student in the classroom.

If the IEP team decides that a student will not take a particular state-or district-wide assessment, the IEP must include an explanation of why that assessment is not appropriate for the student and what assessment is appropriate for the student. This is called an ***alternate assessment***.

A small number of students with significant cognitive disabilities take the Florida Alternate Assessment (FAA). The FAA is for students with disabilities who require direct intensive instruction in skills needed for community living, leisure, and vocational activities.

Criterion-Referenced Tests

Unless otherwise specified, most ESE students are mainstreamed in classes like science and history and are probably taking criterion-referenced assessments. Students may or may not have testing modifications in their IEP, so it is important as the teacher to effectively assess the student.

For example, if a student with an IEP is in a general education history classroom and has a testing accommodation that the test is read to him, the results should accurately depict what the student understands about the content. With the questions being read aloud, the teacher can gauge whether or not the student understands the vocabulary words and content-not if they can read it. The same would hold true if a student were allowed to dictate answers to a paraprofessional. The teacher is still able to assess if the student understands the history information-not if the student can write answers and spell vocabulary correctly.

It is the teacher's responsibility to understand the individual student needs to design appropriate assessments. Although there are multiple delivery methods to criterion referenced testing, it is important to keep the reliability and validity constant with all students. (Dill, 2018)

Standardized Assessment Waiver Process

A student with a disability, for whom the IEP team determines that the statewide standardized assessments cannot accurately measure the student's abilities, taking into consideration all allowable accommodations shall have assessment results waived for the purpose of receiving a course grade and a standard high school diploma. The waiver shall be designated on the student's transcript (Bureau of Exceptional Education and Student Services, 2017, p4).

To be considered for a statewide, standardized assessment results waiver, the following criteria must be met:

- The student must be identified as having a disability
- The student must have an individual education plan (IEP)
- The student must have taken the statewide, standardized assessment with appropriate allowable accommodations at least once
- IEP team must make a determination of whether a statewide, standardized assessment accurately measures the student's abilities

IEP Assessments

There are a number of tests available to diagnose whether a student has an exceptionality and needs to enter exceptional student education. Assessments must pertain to the known or suspected disability. For example, a student suspected of hearing loss would not be given an IQ test and vice versa. The following are the most common IEP assessments given:

- Wechsler Intelligence Scale (WISC-III) – conducted by a school psychologist to measure a student's ability in three intelligence quotient areas: verbal, performance, and full-scale
- Woodcock-Johnson Psychoeducational Battery – given by a special education teacher to measure individual educational development. Helps to identify areas of need of the student so IEP team can create meaningful goals
- Behavior Assessment System for Children (BASC) – a questionnaire given to stakeholders and student to complete. All questionnaires are then compared for behavior and/or mental health problems
- School Function Assessment (SFA) – given by an occupational therapist, this assessment evaluates the student's function in the school environment in the areas of participation, task support, and activity performance
- Clinical Evaluation of Language Fundamentals (CELF) – given by a speech and language pathologist, this assessment tests verbal and written language in order to develop goals for speech therapy

This page is left blank intentionally.

Competency 3
Knowledge of Instructional Practices in Exceptional Student Education

1. Select reliable sources of evidence-based instructional practices and interventions.
2. Apply appropriate instructional approaches, strategies, and materials based on assessments of the student's educational needs (e.g., grade-level standards, academic and functional performance, effect of exceptionality).
3. Choose effective instructional strategies to promote a student's generalization of knowledge and skills across content areas, curriculum, and settings.
4. Identify the characteristics and purposes of the core curriculum, supplemental programs, and intensive interventions as they relate to language arts and mathematics in a multi-tiered system of supports.
5. Apply techniques for differentiating, accommodating, and modifying classroom instruction to meet the educational needs of individual students with exceptionalities.
6. Apply flexible grouping strategies (e.g., academic, behavioral, social) for specific instructional activities.
7. Use criteria for selecting and utilizing print and nonprint media for instructional use to match student needs and interests.
8. Analyze characteristics of specialized instructional approaches for students with significant disabilities.

Competency 3 makes up 21% of the exam or approximately 25 questions.

Evidence-Based Instructional Practices and Interventions

Effective ESE educators use **evidence-based**, sometimes referred to as **research-based**, approaches to make the most effective and appropriate decisions for their students. Evidence base develops when researchers use specific methods to study and instructional approach to see if it works on a large scale. This reduces the risk of making false judgments about how successful the approach is.

There are several types of evidence-based practices, either informal or formal, teachers can use to make decisions in the classroom.

Test Scores

- Example: A teacher uses students' scores on a reading assessment to determine growth. She will then decide whether to continue with the intervention she is using or change methods.

Behavior Data

- Example: A student who is on a Multi-Tiered System of Support (MTSS) has shown improved behavior during reading and math time. The teacher decides to introduce the student to cooperative learning in math class.

Parent Surveys

- A teacher is trying to decide how she will communicate with parents consistently. She sends out a survey to see the parents' communication preferences. She then makes a decision based on what she finds when looking over the survey results.

Observations

- A teacher is walking around the room observing students as they read in cooperative groups. She decides, based on her observation, how to move forward in the lesson.

Peer-Reviewed Academic Journals

- A teacher is regularly reading academic journals that govern her profession, so she can stay abreast on new research and best-practices being used in the field.

Knowledge and Skills Across Content Areas

Integrated curriculum may also be referred to as cross-curricular, interdisciplinary, and multidisciplinary curriculum. In this practice, educators intermingle subject areas. This helps students make connections between and among subjects. For example, a teacher might integrate social studies and English by reading a story about a little girl who launched herself into outer space and then participate in an activity that focuses on the history of US space exploration.

Example of Integrated Curriculum for 10th Grade

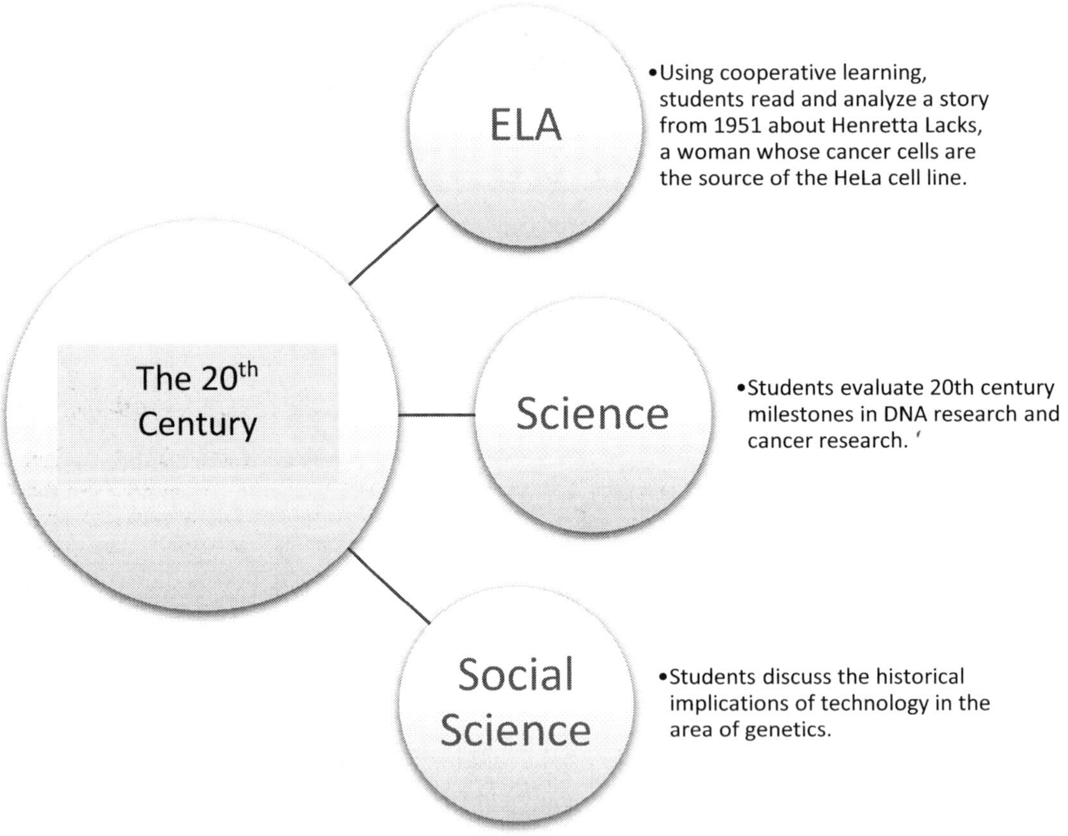

NAVAED

Vertical Alignment

The Florida Standards are vertically aligned—every skill leads to the next skill and the next skill. For example, the skills outlined in the Florida Standards for 7th-grade math are designed to help students prepare for what they will need in 8th-grade math, 9th-grade math, and so on. While the standards are designed to be vertically aligned, it is the responsibility of the educator to ensure students are receiving lessons that are vertically aligned. Educators can vertically align their lessons by:

- collaborating with other teachers in PLCs;
- paying close attention to the standards that come before and after the year being taught; and
- attending professional development that focuses on standards alignment.

Horizontal Alignment

The Florida Standards are also horizontally aligned between and among content areas. For example, the 9th grade social studies teachers plan with the 9th-grade English teachers to design a common lesson focusing on the Civil Rights Movement. This lesson will fulfill social studies standards in U.S. history and English Language Arts standards in reading and writing. This relationship between the two content areas and the focus on common content, goals, and standards make this horizontally aligned. Effective educators can be sure lessons are horizontally aligned by:

- collaborating with other teachers in PLCs;
- researching other content areas that relate to the content being taught; and
- looking for connections where curriculum can support other content areas.

Effective Instructional Strategies for Exceptional Students

The special education teacher is responsible for selecting and using appropriate instructional strategies in the special education classroom. While there are many practical strategies that are effective, it is important that individual student needs and learning styles are taken into consideration. A multi-modal approach (visual, kinesthetic and tactile, and auditory learners) is recommended in order to achieve success. The following strategies serve as examples of effective strategies in the exceptional student education classroom. This is not a definitive list as there are many strategies to choose from, this is a broad generalization (Watson, 2018). When answering questions on the exam, remember to choose strategies that are appropriate to the scenario given.

Classroom Environment

- Seat students in an area free of distraction, reduce visual distraction
- Eliminate all unnecessary materials from student desk
- Use checklists to keep students organized
- Allow student frequent breaks

Time Management and Transition

- Place intermittent breaks between work periods
- Provide additional time to complete assignments
- Use multiple reminders several minutes apart before changing from one activity to the next
- Provide a specific place for turning in assignments

Presentation of Materials

- Modify expectations based on student needs
- Provide a model of the end product

- Provide written and verbal instructions with visuals if possible
- Provide outlines, study guides, and copies of notes
- Explain learning expectations before beginning a lesson
- Make sure students are attentive before giving lesson
- Provide incentives for beginning and completing assignments

Assessment, Grading, and Testing

- Provide a quiet setting
- Divide test into small sections
- Grade spelling separately from content
- Avoid timed test
- Allow for retakes

Behavior

- Avoid confrontations
- Develop a system or code that lets the student know when a behavior is inappropriate
- Ignore attention seeking behaviors that are not disruptive to the classroom
- Develop a set of norms in the classroom and display visually for all students to see
- Provide immediate reinforcers and feedback

A Multi-Tiered System of Supports (MTSS)

Most districts have moved to MTSS when addressing the needs of struggling students. The MTSS framework is evidence-based and has had a significant impact on addressing the needs of struggling subgroups of students (Gordillo, 2015). Students do not have to be classified ESE to receive MTSS.

- MTSS addresses academic as well as the social, emotional, and behavioral development of children from early childhood to graduation (Hurst, 2014).
- MTSS provides multiple levels of support for all learners—struggling through advanced (Hurst, 2014).

MTSS Tiered Systems	
Tier 1	This is the type of modifications or differentiated instruction ***all*** students get in the form of instruction (academic and behavior/social-emotional) and student supports. Tier 1 is the basic and general implementation of the core curriculum that is aligned to the state standards.
Tier 2	This is the type of modifications or differentiated instruction ***some*** students receive in addition to Tier 1 instruction. The purpose of Tier 2 instruction and supports is to improve student performance under Tier 1 performance expectations. This is also referred to as accommodations. The standards and expectations remain the same as Tier 1. However, accommodations are used for these students to be successful.
Tier 3	This is the type of modifications or differentiated instruction ***few*** students receive and is the most intense service level a school can provide to a student. Typically, Tier 3 services are provided to very small groups and/or individual students. The purpose of Tier 3 services is to help students overcome significant barriers to learning academic and/or behavior skills required for school success (Florida's MTSS, n.d.).

MTSS for Mathematics

The following steps offer a tiered approach to mathematics.

Tier 1 – Universal Math Instruction

This instruction level supports all students, including students with disabilities and English language learners. High quality, evidence-based instructional practices are delivered with fidelity in recognition of student strengths. Screening and progress monitoring is used to determine if the instruction is effective for most students.

Tier 2 – Supplemental Math Interventions

Use of supplemental interventions and data analysis to determine whether an intervention is working to improve the outcome for at-risk students in math. It includes distinguishing features of supplemental interventions and considerations for selecting and implementing evidence-based math interventions to effectively address student skill deficits in mathematics. Progress-monitoring strategies are used to determine if the student is responding to interventions accordingly before intensifying instruction.

Tier 3 – Intensive Math Interventions

Data-based individualization is used to increase the intensity of math interventions to accommodate the individual needs of non-responding students. This will identify strategies for intensifying math instruction to appropriately address the student's severe and persistent learning needs. This step uses more frequent and precise progress monitoring to determine if adequate gains in math are being made with the specially designed instruction.

(CEEDAR Center, 2015)

MTSS for Language Arts

Tier 1

This tier encompasses the core instruction of language arts. The teacher will model a specific writing skill that students will learn during instruction. The goal is to have students imitate the important components of the targeted writing skill. Provide students with consistent, predictable writing times to allow them to develop writing skills. Encourage students to collaborate with each other with specific instructions and modeling and allow for opportunities of revising their work. Finally, provide students with frequent and specific feedback.

Tier 2

This tier incorporates a self-regulated approach for writing which is a framework of teaching stages for writing skills and strategies to help student learn about the writing process. Strategies include goal setting, self-monitoring, self-assessment, self-instruction, and self-reinforcement. The purpose is to motivate and empower students to become good writers. Following independent practice and feedback, allow students the opportunity to revise and improve their writing.

Tier 3

This tier incorporates a framework of teaching strategies to help students how to compose simple messages, acquire foundational concepts about print, articulate words slowly to hear and record letters in words to communicate a message, write letters fluently, and build a core of high-frequency words. In this intervention, communication remains a purpose and the writing is always meaningful. The writing is also used to draw attention to details of printed words in order to reinforce and extend the student's word identification skills and apply reading strategies to predict and monitor reading.

(Madison Metropolitan School District, 2014)

Techniques for Differentiating, Accommodating, and Modifying Instruction

Differentiation in the classroom does not mean providing separate unrelated activities for each and every individual student. Differentiation provides interrelated activities that are based on student needs for the purpose of ensuring that all students come to a similar grasp of a skill or idea. This form of instruction helps students with diverse academic needs and learning styles master the same challenging academic content.

The following techniques are used as examples of how to meet the educational needs of students with exceptionalities through differentiation, accommodations, and modifications.

- Provide extra time to complete assignments and take tests
- Give a modified assignment that is shorter or different
- Provide specific feedback more frequently than other students
- Provide slower paced instruction
- Provide physical adaptations
- Provide a note-taker or another assistant to the student
- Allow the use of a computer for certain assignments
- Digitalized books and class materials
- Preferential seating
- Allow breaks often and in between lessons
- Provide student with a home set of class materials

Although there are many techniques, it is important to have an understanding that the goal of the teacher is to meet the needs of the exceptional student in whatever way possible in order for them to show proficiency and mastery of the state-adopted standards.

(Center for Parent Information and Resources, 2017)

Flexible Grouping

Flexible grouping can be used to accommodate students with different interests and abilities. Teachers should continuously switch student groups based on different needs or preferences students have at any given time. Flexible grouping is a term that covers a wide range of grouping students for delivering instruction such as whole class, small group, and a partner.

- To maximize student performance instruction is provided in flexible groupings. Heterogeneous grouping is used when objectives are appropriate for the range of learners in the classroom. Homogeneous grouping is used to customize specific instruction for assessed student needs.
    - ***Homogeneous Groups.*** Everyone is the same. For example, a group of all level 3 readers. Homogenous groups should not be used regularly. **Done mostly with EBD students**.
    - ***Heterogeneous Groups.*** Diversity within the group. For example, grouping students by interest rather than reading scores will provide more diversity among the group members.
- Group size and composition are adjusted to accommodate and reflect student progress and instructional objectives.
- Tutoring with a peer, adult, or both are used to supplement explicit teacher-delivered instruction. The practice should align with classroom objectives and instruction.
- Cross-class or cross-grade grouping is used when appropriate to maximize opportunities to tailor instruction to students' performance levels. This is appropriate when teaching students within a similar age span and achievement range.

- Centers and independent activities should be aligned with instructional goals and objectives focused on achieving grade-level standards.

Print and Non-print Media

The selection and use of print and non-print media depend upon how well their significance accommodates instruction as well as how it fits into the learning environment. The following must be taken into consideration when choosing print and non-print media.

- **Relevance –** Select only materials that make a distinct contribution to the identified learning objectives. The media chosen must have relevance to the content being taught.
- **Choice –** Students must be able to self-select texts based on interest. Be sure you have an array of relevant material for students to choose.
- **Planning –** It is imperative teachers know the level of student receiving instruction; this is especially important for students with disabilities. Appropriateness is key when dealing with students with visual disabilities, such as using large print and braille.
- **Visibility –** The media chosen must be easily accessible to all learners in the classroom environment. All words must be correctly spelled, well written, and appropriately spaced for easy visibility. The students must be in a position to see the type of media being used and must be able to utilize the provided material adequately.

Instructional Approaches for Students with Significant Disabilities

Students with severe handicaps will often have minimal ability in some areas. It is important to remember these students have a right to be included and to have their needs met. The following approaches are recommended when educating the severely disabled:

- Use grade-appropriate materials as much as possible.
- Be consistent and have predictable routines for everything done in the classroom.
- Be explicit when giving directions and outline exactly what the student is supposed to do for each task.
- Identify clear goals and expectations. Stay vigilant as success may take a great deal of time. Celebrate achievements, no matter how small.
- Make sure everything is relevant to the student with whom you are working.
- Track progress carefully in order to define when the student is ready for the next milestone.
- Teach skills in a variety of settings because these students do not generalize.
- Once a student accomplishes a goal/task, be sure to use the skill regularly to ensure mastery continues on.

(Watson, 2019)

This page is left blank intentionally.

Competency 4
Knowledge of the Positive Behavioral Support Process

1. Identify and choose appropriate prevention and intensive intervention strategies for students who display challenging behaviors.
2. Distinguish the various concepts and models of positive behavior support.
3. Analyze the legal and ethical issues pertaining to positive behavior support strategies and disciplinary procedures for students with exceptionalities.
4. Interpret individual and group data to apply interventions that increase positive behavior.
5. Interpret the essential elements of a functional behavior assessment and measure the effects of the behavior intervention plan through data collection strategies.

This competency makes up 12% of the exam or approximately 14 questions.

Student Behavior

Student behavior should be approached the same way student learning is approached. Teachers must observe behavior, collect data on that behavior, and then devise a plan of action. Sending students to detention does not fix a behavior problem. Learning about the behavior and differentiating the approach to the behavior is most effective.

Behavior Tips:

- ***Observe the behavior first.*** Before a teacher can prescribe punishment or a solution to the behavior, she must first observe the behavior. These observations yield necessary data the teacher should consider before moving forward.
- ***Come up with a plan.*** Using an evidenced-based approach, begin to design a plan of action. Allow the student to be a part of behavior plans. Allowing students to set behavior goals and devise a plan on how to attain them helps students take ownership of the process.
- ***Contracts work.*** Using positive language, come up with an agreement you and the student can live by. Help the student outline a goal. Let the student be part of the construction of the contract. Revisit the contract to celebrate gains and to make new goals.

Adolescent Behavior

Adolescence is a time for developing independence. Adolescents typically exercise their independence by questioning, and sometimes breaking, the rules. During this time students are trying to develop an identity, gain acceptance from peers, and measure up to develop competence. The most common function of behavior displayed by adolescents is avoidance coping, or avoidance behaviors. Avoidance behaviors are ways of behaving that are motivated by the desire to avoid certain thoughts or feelings. The behaviors will include avoiding places or situations such as school or social events.

Positive & Effective Classroom Behavioral Management System

Most districts have moved from a top-down, punitive system of dealing with behavior, to a restorative justice, positive behavior management system. The research shows that positive behavior support yields better results than a system focused on punishments.

> **Quick Tip!**
> When looking at test questions having to do with student behavior, any answer choice that sounds negative or punitive is probably ***NOT*** the correct answer choice.

Positive Behavior Support (PBS). PBS is a set of research-based strategies used to increase quality of life and decrease problem behavior by teaching new skills and making changes in a person's environment (Association for Positive Behavior Support, 2018).

PBS includes tiered intervention systems. Positive behavior support focuses on the positive behaviors rather than punishing the negative behaviors.

Behavioral Data Collection. Data-driven decision making is when a teacher collects data, analyzes the data, and then makes a decision based on the data. Observing a behavior before deciding how to move forward is data-driven decision making. Observations, journal entries, surveys, interviews, etc. yield important information teachers can use to be effective when applying intervention strategies.

Positive Behavior Support Strategies

Focusing on the positive when engaging with students and managing behavior is key. Students respond positively to specific and meaningful feedback. Making sure to specifically praise students for appropriate behavior will help them to want to continue acting in a positive manner. A teacher can enhance positive behavior by:

Setting clear expectations. Teachers should be explicit when communicating academic and behavioral expectations. Rubrics are effective tools in setting expectations for behavior, assignments, and classroom activities.

Use evidence-based practices. Before choosing programs and plans of action in the classroom, teachers must research the effectiveness of these programs. There should be evidence to support the use of the program.

Focusing on positive aspects of behavior. By rewarding positive behavior, students will strive to do more positive things. Constantly yelling and reprimanding students leads to frustration for students and teachers.

Celebrating gains in academics and behavior. When students meet a milestone or have an academic gain, celebrate. When students receive accolades for good behavior and academic gains, they will continue to strive.

Focusing on the intrinsic value of achieving. Intrinsic value means the student is doing something because for him or herself and not for an extrinsic reward. Intrinsic value helps students to stay motivated to do positive things. Candy and parties are extrinsic motivators that work; however, extrinsic rewards will eventually stop working. For real change to occur in student behavior, students must understand the intrinsic rewards for effectively managing their behavior. Once a student can learn to feel good about accomplishments throughout the day, he or she will strive to continue to make good choices.

Decide with data. Information should be collected, reviewed, and acted upon routinely, formally, and directly using key questions:

- What topic or problem needs to be addressed when, where, and how?
- What intervention or practice best addresses the need or problem?
- How well is the intervention or practice being implemented?
- How well are students responding?
- What adjustments are needed to improve fidelity and student responsiveness?

Cultural Relevance. Development and implementation of behavior support practices must explicitly reflect the cultural learning history of students, staff, family, and community members. This includes language, customs and practices, normative expectations, and forms of acknowledgments and recognition. Systems tailored to these needs are more likely to be effective than those implemented in a generic form.

Positive Behavior Support Models

School-Wide Positive Behavior Support (SW-PBS)

This model refers to multi-tiered applications of Positive Behavior Support in schools K through 12 with an emphasis on preventative strategies at universal, secondary, and tertiary levels. It is designed to enhance school climate and promote improved behavioral, social, and academic outcomes. Practices are organized into three tiers

1. **Universal Practices –** intended for the entire school population
2. **Secondary/Targeted Practices –** intended for high-risk segments of the population
3. **Tertiary Practices –** individualized and intensive strategies focused on students who already present with serious challenges in need of intervention

Pyramid Model

The Pyramid Model is an example of program-wide Positive Behavior Support. It was developed to promote young children's social-emotional competence and address challenging behavior. The model is a framework comprised of evidence-based practices organized into three tiers: **prevention, promotion,** and **intervention**. The Pyramid Model is designed to meet the needs and contexts of programs serving infants, toddlers, and preschoolers.

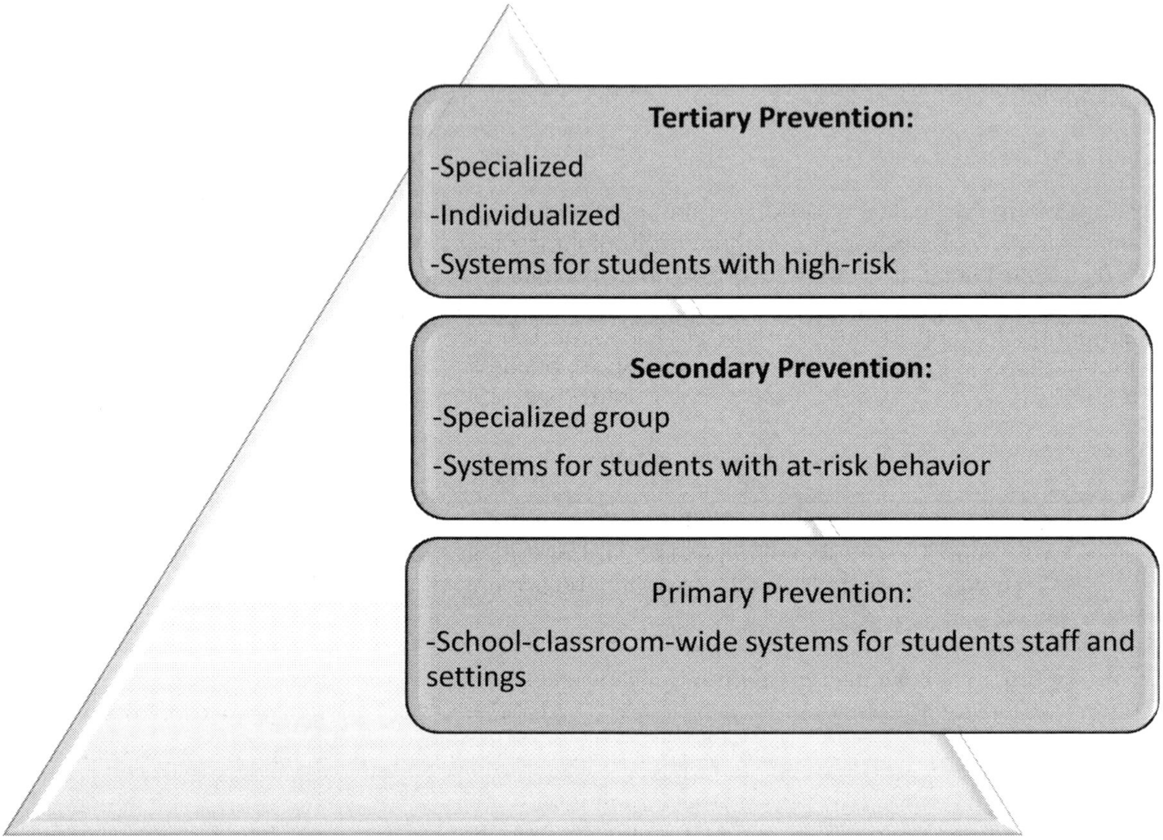

(Adapted from Dunlap & Fox, 2015)

Positive Self-Concept & Self-Esteem

Students who feel good about themselves will take chances in their learning and stretch beyond their comfort zones. Students who feel like failures all the time will often lack the motivation to work in an academic setting. They will often say, "I will just fail anyway, so why try?" Effective educators help students build positive self-concepts so students can achieve both behaviorally and academically.

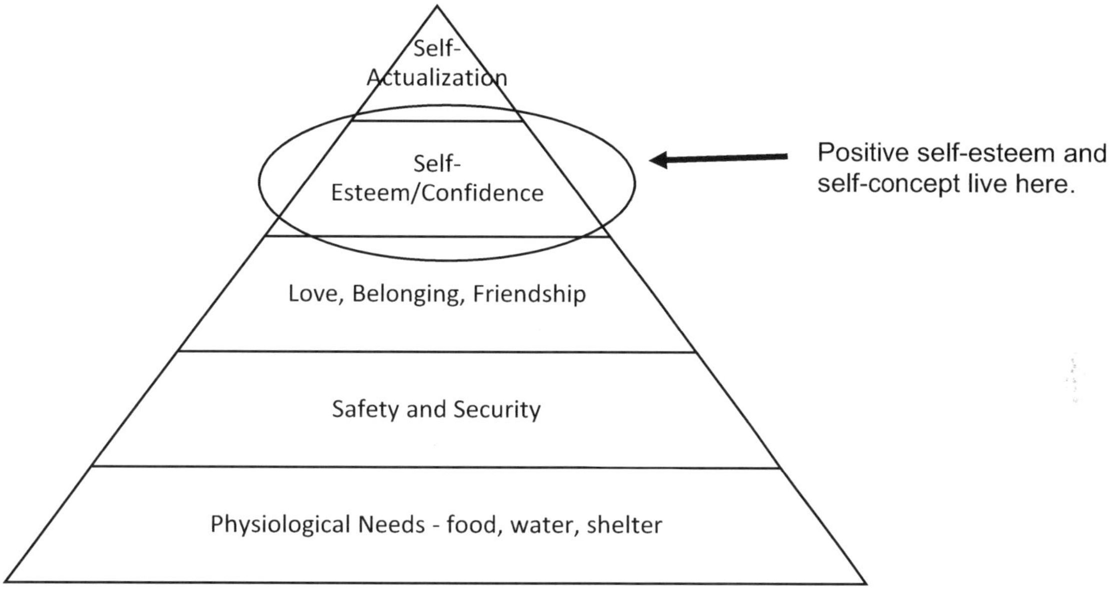

(Maslow)

Ethics in Positive Behavior Support

Behavior support encourages students to change their behavior. Before and during any change in process, the following ethical issues must be considered:

- **Model appropriate leadership –** Educators' behaviors must be seen as positive to the students and to develop a relationship of genuine caring, trust, and respect. Students will model the behavior of leaders in the school.
- **Self-discipline –** Educators should encourage self-discipline as a goal of behavior management. By building respect and trust, the student will feel the need to control his/her behavior.
- **Show empathy –** Empathy is the ability to understand and share feelings together. Educators must consider the students' problems objectively and in an empathetic manner.
- **Freedom and independence to function –** Students should be allowed as much independence as possible to function. If limits need to be established to avoid injury, limits should be set keeping in mind that students should experience the logical consequences of their actions in order to develop self-reliance and independence.
- **Principle of normalization –** The student must be allowed to function in as normal an environment as possible.
- **Principle of fairness –** An intervention must be fair and allow the student to succeed in school. If consequences are applied, they must be appropriate regarding the degree of the offense.
- **Principle of respect and dignity –** An intervention must provide the opportunity for a student to learn or improve a skill without degrading the individual as a human being.

- **Continuum of behavior management interventions –** Educators should use the most effective intervention with the least restrictions to the student in the classroom. Over-restricting often imposes on students' rights within the classroom.
- **Behavior change must be rational and well planned –** the behavior must be one which hampers the student's performance in the classroom. To change the behavior the educator must have a rationale for changing the behavior and follow a behavioral change procedure. The result is an implementation of a behavioral strategy that is prescriptive to the behavior and does not violate ethical considerations or due process.
- **Consent –** To avoid conflict over behavior intervention, educators should notify stakeholders involved with the student. Educators must obtain consent to proceed.

Manifestation

If a student's misbehavior is a result of his or her disability, the misbehavior is called a "manifestation" of the disability. For example, Susan has been diagnosed with a behavior disability. She often lashes out in class and can be disruptive. In this case, the school cannot suspend Susan because of her outbursts because the outbursts and disruptiveness are a manifestation of her disability. Instead, the IEP team develops protocols for behavior interventions for Susan.

Manifestation Determination Review. If a student is facing consequences such school suspension, school administration will conduct a manifestation determination review. In this meeting, the team decides if a student's misbehavior is a result of his or her disability.

According to the Florida Department of Education (2012), if a student is suspended out of school for more than 10 days in a row or an accumulation of 10 days in a school year, the following must happen:

1. The school must provide services during student removal. The IEP team decides which services the student needs.
2. The IEP team must meet to develop a plan for carrying out a **functional behavioral assessment** and for developing a **behavioral intervention plan** (if one has not been done) or to review the existing plan and its implementation and change it as needed.
3. The IEP team must carry out a ***manifestation determination review*** within 10 school days of any decision to change the placement of a student with disabilities because of a violation of a code of student conduct.
    a. If the misbehavior **is not** due to the student's disability, the student may be disciplined in the same way as a student without a disability, but the student must continue to receive educational services during the removal.
    b. If the misbehavior **is** due to the student's disability and did not involve weapons, drugs, or serious bodily injury to the student or others, the school may return the student to their current placement or the school may choose to change the child's placement using the IEP team's regular change of placement procedures.
    c. If the misbehavior **is** due to the student's disability and involved weapons, drugs, or serious bodily injury, the IEP team determines an interim alternative educational setting.
    d. If the misbehavior **is** due to the student's disability and a ***hearing officer*** determines the student may be dangerous to herself or others, school personnel will recommend an interim alternative placement to a hearing officer, who makes the placement decision.

Seclusion and Restraint on Students with Disabilities

All school districts to have policies and procedures in place for monitoring the use of seclusion and restraint. **Seclusion** is defined as the involuntary confinement of a student alone in a room or area from which the student is physically prevented from leaving. The purpose is to calm the student by placing him/her in a non-locked setting under supervision.

There are two types of restraint. **Mechanical restraint** is the use of any device or equipment that restricts a student's freedom of movement. **Physical restraint** is a physical force immobilizing or reducing the ability of a student to move his/her torso, arms, legs, or head freely.

Anytime a student is placed in seclusion or under restraint, it must be documented in an incident report. Schools are required to notify the parents/guardians in writing the same day that the incident occurs. If requested, an incident report must be mailed within three days and include all the information on the incident.

Functional Behavior Assessment (FBA)

According to IDEA Partnership (n.d.) a functional behavior assessment is a comprehensive and individualized strategy to identify the purpose or function of a student's problem behavior(s), develop and implement a plan to modify variables that maintain the problem behavior, and teach appropriate replacement behaviors using positive interventions.

There are 5 steps to a functional behavior assessment.

> **Quick Tip!**
> Data is a key component in any plan for behavior. Observations are a form of data. Teachers must use data to drive classroom decisions. This includes behavior data.

1. **Define target behavior –** Through the use of interview, school records, behavior observation data, incident reports, and any other appropriate methods, identify the most severe and difficult behavior as the target behavior
2. **Collect data –** Collect measurable and observational data by direct observation of the target behavior in the environment in which it occurs. Charting, narrative data, rating scales, school records, narrative documentation, and academic performance are acceptable to use.
3. **Develop a hypothesis –** With the collected data, an hypothesis about the function or purpose of the target behavior is made. The intervention plan will help reject or refine the hypothesis and allow for revision if necessary.
4. **Planning interventions –** a *behavioral intervention plan* (BIP) is developed identifying new skills to be taught, modifications made to environment and instructional delivery, accommodations to curriculum, and changes in behavior management strategies. The BIP indicates who is responsible for implementation and monitoring the effect of the plan.
5. **Evaluate effectiveness of plan –** Data relevant to the target behavior is collected and compared to baseline data. If data is favorable the intervention continues. If data is not favorable, return to step 1 and revaluate target behavior. Continue the entire process all over again until an effective plan is created.

Proximity Control

Proximity control is an effective way to address off-task behaviors (talking, not paying attention, working on another task). As the teacher moves around her room, she can move herself close to the student(s) who is (are) engaging in undesirable behavior. Usually the nearness of the teacher shuts the behavior down. It is nonconfrontational and does not disrupt the teaching/learning process.

The answer is NEVER going to be something that causes the student embarrassment, shames a student, or disrupts instruction.

Off-Task Scenarios

1) David is whispering to Myra as Mr. Jackson is delivering a brief lesson on the causes of the Civil War before students break up into small groups. What is a good first step to get the students back on task?

2) Jason is tapping his pencil on his desk during a test. Mrs. Rodriguez can see that other students are becoming agitated. What should she do?

3) Miranda is nodding off while she is supposed to be taking notes on a video of a speech. How can Ms. Williams get Miranda on task in a nonverbal, nonconfrontational way?

PROXIMITY CONTROL!

Extinction

A procedure when reinforcement of a previously rewarded behavior is halted is called **extinction.** More commonly referred to as planned ignoring, extinction does not require the use of punishment procedures to decrease problem behavior. Extinction requires withholding of reinforcement by ignoring behavior, denying access to tangible items or activities, not allowing the learner to escape or avoid a non-preferred task or situation, and/or preventing reinforcing sensory feedback.

Pre-Correction

A strategy in which the teacher verbally, gesturally, or physically prompts a student to respond with the correct response to a question or event is called **pre-correction.** When using pre-correction, the teacher identifies the task or behavior and explicitly teaches the student the correct response. Having knowledge of the academic patterns and behaviors, the teacher identifies when target responses should occur. This is most notably useful when creating or amending a behavioral intervention plan.

Competency 5
Knowledge of Multiple Literacies and Communication Skills

1. Identify language development and the components of language structure.
2. Distinguish characteristics of communication disorders and the impact on academic achievement and functional skills.
3. Identify appropriate assistive technology and alternative communication systems to facilitate communication across all educational settings.
4. Determine the sequence of reading development and the critical components of reading proficiency included in the state standards.
5. Apply specialized instructional strategies and techniques to address deficits in phonological processing in students with exceptionalities.
6. Apply evidence-based instructional methods for increasing reading proficiency in phonics, word recognition, and fluency that meet the specific educational and functional needs of individual students with exceptionalities.
7. Apply evidence-based instructional methods for increasing literacy (e.g., oral language, vocabulary, reading comprehension) in all content areas that meet the specific educational and functional needs of individual students with exceptionalities.
8. Determine and apply strategies for facilitating students' critical-thinking, executive functioning, and metacognition skills.
9. Select and use effective instructional methods and supports for teaching writing foundations, the writing process, and purposes of writing to meet specific educational and functional needs of individual students with exceptionalities across all content areas.
10. Apply evidence-based instructional methods for increasing mathematic skills in all content areas that meet the specific educational and functional needs of individual students with exceptionalities.

Competency 4 makes up 22% of the exam or approximately 26 questions.

Components of Language

There are five basic components found across all languages. Language acquisition progresses across these components with increasing quantity, first with sounds then words then sentence length. The five components are described below.

Language Component	Description
Phonology	Speech structure within a language including both the patterns of basic speech units and the accepted rules of pronunciation is known as phonology. The smallest units of sounds are called **phonemes**. For example, the word "that" contains three phonemes. The "th" represents one phoneme /th/, the "a" is a short a sound /a/, and the "t" is its basic sound /t/.
Morphology	The smallest units of meanings are called **morphemes.** Morphemes include base words such as "cat," "hot," or "dove," as well as affixes such as "un-," "re-," the plural "s" or "es," and the past tense "ed." Morphology is a critical component to vocabulary development and represents the building blocks for comprehension.
Syntax	The process in which individual words and their most basic meaningful units combine to create a sentence is known as **syntax.** For example, "I went to the store" is a meaningful sentence with proper syntax while "To store went I" is not proper English.
Semantics	Semantics refers to the ways in which language coveys meaning. Semantics moves beyond literal meaning of words and is culture-dependent, which is why it is the most difficult components of language for individuals who are not native speakers or from different cultures. For example, to wish someone good luck by saying "break a leg" does not literally mean go out and break a leg.
Pragmatics	Pragmatics is the element that connects all language components and is the contextual and social use of linguistics. It focuses on the communication in language rather than structure by going beyond the literal meaning to consider how it is constructed as well as focusing on implied meaning. For example, the way we speak to our parents is different than speaking with a group of friends or the language used in a formal speech is different than the language used in a fairytale. Knowing the difference and when to use each style is pragmatics.

Characteristics of Communication Disorders

Communication disorders occur when there is an impairment in the ability to receive, send, process, and comprehend concepts or verbal, nonverbal, and graphic symbols. These disorders may be evident in hearing, language, and/or speech and range in severity from mild to profound. Whether the disorder is developmental or acquired, individuals may demonstrate one or any combination of communication disorders that result in a primary disability or secondary to other disabilities.

Speech disorder – an impairment of the articulation of speech sounds, fluency, and/or voice.

- **Articulation disorder** – atypical production of speech sounds characterized by substitutions, omissions, additions, or distortions that may interfere with intelligibility.
- **Fluency disorder** – Interruption in the flow of speaking characterized by atypical rate, rhythm, and repetitions in sounds, syllables, words, and phases. Excessive tension, struggle behavior, and secondary mannerisms are also characteristics of this disorder.
- **Voice disorder** – abnormal production and/or absences of vocal quality, pitch, loudness, resonance, and/or duration which is inappropriate for an individual's age and/or sex.

Language disorder – Impaired comprehension and/or use of spoken, written, and/or other symbol systems. This disorder may involve the form (phonology, morphology, syntax), content (semantics), and/or function (pragmatics) of language in communication in any combination.

Hearing disorder – Impaired auditory sensitivity of the physiological auditory system. This may limit the development, comprehension, production, and/or maintenance of speech and/or language. Hearing disorders are classified according to difficulties in detection, recognition, discrimination, comprehension, and perception of auditory information.

- **Deaf** – hearing disorder that limits and individual's aural/oral communication performance to the extent that the primary sensory input for communication may be other than the auditory channel.
- **Hard of hearing** – hearing disorder that is fluctuating or permanent which affects an individual's ability to communicate. Hard-of-hearing individuals rely on the auditory channel as the primary sensory input for communication.

Central Auditory Processing Disorders – deficits in the information processing of audible signals not attributed to impaired peripheral hearing sensitivity or intellectual impairment. CAPD refers to limitations in the ongoing transmission, analysis, organization, transformation, elaboration, storage, retrieval, and use of information contained in audible signals. The following are characteristics of CAPD:

- Inability to store and retrieve information efficiently
- Filter, sort, and combine information at inappropriate perceptual and conceptual levels
- Failure to attend, discriminate, and identify acoustic signals
- Inability to transform and transmit information through peripheral and central nervous systems
- Failure to attach meaning to a stream of acoustic signals through the use of linguistic and nonlinguistic contexts

(American Speech-Language-Hearing Association, 1993)

Alternate Communication and Assistive Technology

Alternate Communication

Augmentative/Alternative communication refers to any mode of communication other than speech. This includes systems such as sign language, symbol or picture boards, and electronic devices with synthesized speech. **Augmentative** systems are used by people who have some speech but are unintelligible or have limited abilities to use their speech. **Alternative** communication is when a person has no speech. There are two types of systems used to facilitate communication.

- **Unaided systems** – using your own body to include gestures, body language, facial expression, and sign language.
- **Aided systems** – using some type of tool or device and is either basic or high-tech. Pointing to pictures, letters, or words on a board is a basic system. Touching letters or pictures on a computer screen that speaks to you is high tech.

Assistive Technology

Low technology devices or systems include dry erase boards, binders, folders, albums, and other means to store or convey images or pictures used in the communication process.

Mid-technology devices or systems include tape recorders, overhead projectors, and simple voice output communication aids.

High technology devices or systems include computers, software, adaptive hardware and keyboards, and more complex voice output communication aids.

Critical Components of Reading

There are five critical components of reading.

Phonemic Awareness

Phonemic awareness is the knowledge that words are made up of a combination of individual sounds and also includes the ability to hold on to those sounds, blend them successfully into words, and take them apart again. The smallest unit of sound in a word is called a **phoneme.** For example, *cat* is made up of three phonemes (sounds) /c/ /a/ and /t/. When the three sounds are combined fluidly, they make the word *cat.* If a student knows that *cat, car,* and *cabbage* all have the same sound at the beginning of the word, then they have phonemic awareness.

Phonics

Phonics is the relationship between a specific letter and its sound as it relates to the written word. For example, a student will use phonics when faced with an unknown word while reading. By focusing on the specific sound of each letter or combination of letters, the student will break the word into pieces assigning the appropriate sound to each in order to decode the word.

Fluency

Fluency is the ability to read text accurately and smoothly with expression, intonation, and pacing to sound natural—much like speaking. Fluency depends on higher word recognition skills so that less energy is wasted on deciphering words and more is spent on comprehending what is read. The only way to improve fluency is to practice. Re-reading familiar texts several times, unison reading, modeling fluent reading, and choral reading are effective fluency strategies.

Vocabulary

Vocabulary skills increase through direct and indirect instruction. Students continuously learn new words through listening and speaking to people around them, reading on their own, and being read to by others. Some new words must be taught explicitly due to the fact they might be crucial to understanding a story or concept. It is not necessary to understand every word on a page, but too many new or difficult words hinder comprehension.

Comprehension

Comprehension is the intentional thinking process that occurs as we read. Good readers are purposeful using a variety of strategies to create meaning from text. Successful readers also monitor their comprehension by utilizing strategies when reading is understood and when it is not, use prior knowledge, make predictions, question what was read, recognize story structure, and summarize.

> **Quick Tip!**
>
> Students with ADHD often struggle with reading comprehension because ADHD can interfere with processing information.

(National Reading Panel, 2016)

▼ **Pre-Alphabetic Phase**
Students read words by memorizing visual features or guessing words from context.

▼ **Partial-Alphabetic Phase**
Students recognize some letters and can use them to remember words by sight.

▼ **Full-Alphabetic Phase**
Readers possess extensive working knowledge of the graphophonemic system, and they can use this knowledge to analyze fully the connections between graphemes and phonemes in words. They can decode unfamiliar words and store fully analyzed sight words in memory.

▼ **Consolidated-Alphabetic Phase**
Students consolidate their knowledge of grapheme-phoneme blends into larger units that recur in different words.

Word recognition develops in the following phases: pre-alphabetic, partial-alphabetic, full-alphabetic, consolidated-alphabetic (Ehri, 1999).

Phonological awareness is the ability of the reader to recognize the sound of spoken language, including how sounds can be blended together, segmented (divided up), and manipulated (switched around).

- ***Phonemic Awareness.*** Understanding the individual sounds — **phonemes —** in words. For example, for a student to be able to separate the sounds in the word *cat* into three distinct **phonemes**: /k/, /æ/, and /t/.
- ***Phonics/Graphophonic.*** Understanding correspondence between these sounds and the spelling patterns (graphemes) that represent them. **Spelling** is phonics/graphophonics.

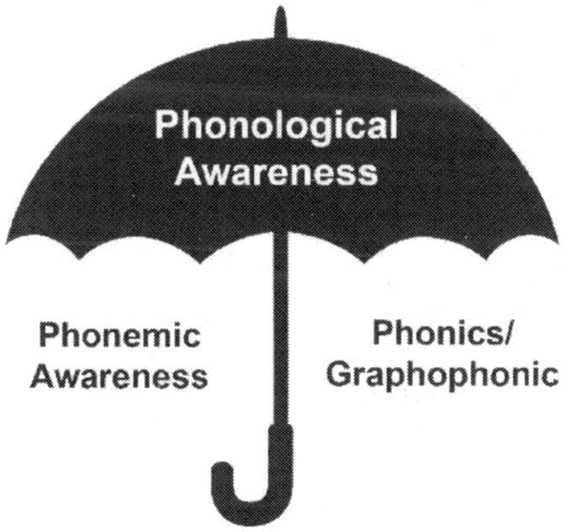

Deficits in Phonological Processing

Phonological disorders refer to the difficulty of understanding the sound system and speech rules of the language that normal functioning students acquire naturally. These disorders are broad in scope and more complex than simple articulation deficits.

Speech-language pathologists (SLPs) diagnose phonological disorders using standard speech assessments as well as clinical observations. The disorders are characterized as slight, mild, moderate, or severe which helps the SLP determine which therapy approaches are most effective.

A student with a phonological disorder may pronounce **/s/** in *sock* clearly, but the **/s/** in *bus* may be dropped and pronounced *bush.* Words with two or more syllables may be pronounced with fewer syllables—*elephant* may be pronounced *ephant.* Whole groups of sounds may be mispronounced the same way. For example, *s, f, sh,* and *ch* sounds may be pronounced as a *t, fire* becomes *tire, shoe* becomes *too,* etc.

After a diagnosis of a phonological disorder, an SLP will put together a therapy plan according to the following pattern of errors:

- Student leaves off the first or last sound in a word
- Student has difficulty producing sounds made at the back of the mouth
- Student stops sounds the should normally continue
- Student leaves off one of the sounds in a consonant blend

(Encyclopedia of Mental Disorders, 2012)

Fluent Readers

Students at this stage have fluency and prosody. **Fluency** is reading without having to stop and decode (sound out) words. Fluency involves reading a paragraph from start to finish with very few errors. **Prosody** is reading with expression while using the words and punctuation correctly. Reading with prosody means the reader is conveying what is on the page, pausing at commas and periods, and using inflection based on punctuation.

Teachers perform **fluency checks** or **fluency reads** to gauge students' reading progress. While the student reads, the teacher follows along. As the student reads, the teacher checks for **automaticity**, or how automatically the student reads. Is the student decoding too often? Can the student automatically say words as she moves down the passage? The teacher also checks the student's **accuracy** and **rate**.

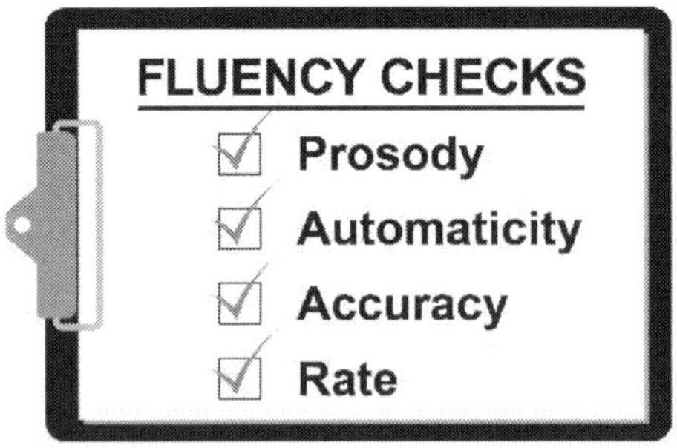

Teaching strategies to increase and monitor fluency:

- ***Choral Reading.*** Reading aloud in unison with a whole class or group of students. Choral reading helps build students' fluency, self-confidence, and motivation.
- ***Repeated Reading.*** Reading passages again and again, aiming to read more words correctly per minute each time.
- ***Running Records.*** Following along as a student reads and marking when he or she makes a mistake or **miscues**.
- ***Miscue Analysis.*** Looking over the running record, analyzing why the student miscued. and employing strategies to help the student with miscues.

Scenario: A teacher is following along as a student is reading. The teacher makes a mark whenever the student struggles or incorrectly says a word. After the student is finished reading, both the teacher and the student look over the miscues and discuss why the student miscued and how they can fix the problem. This is a ***fluency read***, a ***running record***, and a ***miscue analysis***.

Methods for Increased Literacy

Structural analysis is the process of interpreting word parts that make up a word. This helps the reader determine the pronunciation and meaning of unknown words. This word identification technique is effective, especially when used along with phonic analysis and context clues. Students can break down the word using its structure.

- ***Compound Words.*** Two words put together (mailman, sidewalk).
- ***Prefixes.*** Additions to root words that help to form a new word with another meaning from that of the root word. Prefixes are at the beginning of a word.
  - *Example: Prefixes that indicate not: un-(unknown), dis- (disregard), im-(impossible), in-(inaccurate), mis-(misunderstand), and ir-(irrational).*
- ***Suffixes.*** Additions to root words that form a new word with another meaning from that of the root word. Suffixes are at the end of a word. They change the part of speech (past tense, present tense) or verb tense of a word. They also indicate whether the word is plural or singular.
  - *Example: -ed, -ing, and plural -s are all suffixes*

> ***Scenario:*** Students are decoding words using the prefixes and suffixes to determine pronunciation and meaning. The students are engaging in a ***structural analysis***. A teacher models how to break down compound words to understand the meaning of the words. The teacher and students are performing a ***structural analysis***.

Words can be broken down by:

- inflected forms (*-s, -es, -ed, -ing, -ly*)
- contractions
- possessives
- compound words
- syllables
- base words
- root words
- prefixes
- suffixes beginning consonants
- end consonants
- medial consonants
- consonant blends (*bl, gr, sp*)
- consonant digraphs (*sh, th, ch*)
- short vowels
- long vowels
- vowel pairs (*oo, ew, oi, oy*)

Blending is an important skill beginners use to mimic the process readers go through to sound out a word as in /p/-/a/-/t/ /pat/.

- ***Onsets.*** Beginning consonant and consonant cluster.
- **Rimes.** Vowel and consonants that follow. Some common rimes are: -ack, -an, -aw, -ick, -ing, -op, -unk, -ain, -ank, -ay, -ide, -ink, -or, -ock, -ight, -ame, -eat, -ine.

> ***Etymology*** is the study of the origins of words and how they have changed over time. If students are analyzing root words and their meaning, they are using etymology.

Sight words are words that do not follow the rules. Students cannot use standard decoding and structure analysis on **sight words.** Students have to memorize sight words.

- want
- what
- why
- said
- see
- there
- by
- are

Scenario: A teacher is helping her students memorize words like *why*, *where*, and *there*. The students are using memorization for their sight words so they can read more fluently.

Comprehension and Critical Thinking

Comprehension is the essence of reading. This is when students begin to form images in their minds as they read. They are able to predict what might happen next in a story because they understand what is happening in the story. Students who are in the comprehension stage of reading do not need to decode (sound out) words. They read **fluently** with **prosody**, **automaticity**, and **accuracy**.

Critical thinking is a high-level cognitive skill. This is when students can apply certain concepts to their reading. They may be able to come up with their own ending of the story or even an extra scene. This is when they are thinking deeply using evaluation and analysis in their reading.

Scenario: A teacher wants students to understand the book she is reading to the class. She stops to think aloud and talk out certain aspects of the story as she reads. She is using a ***read aloud/think aloud*** technique to increase students' ***metacognition***, ***critical thinking***, and ***comprehension***.

Metacognition is thinking about thinking. When students have metacognition, they understand the processes in their minds and can employ a variety of techniques to understand text. Strategies for boosting **comprehension**, **critical thinking**, and **metacognition** are:

- ***Predicting.*** Asking students what they think will happen next.
- ***Questioning.*** Having students ask questions based on what they are reading.
- ***Read aloud/think aloud.*** Teacher or student reads and stops to think aloud about what the text means.
- ***Summarizing.*** Asking students to summarize what they just read in their own words.

*All of these strategies can be employed before, during, and after reading.

Quick Tip!

To be considered an independent reader, a student must read at >95% accuracy.

Allowing students to respond and express themselves as they engage in text is a big part of the reading process. This can be done in a variety of engaging ways through written and oral activities.

Student Response to Text

Activity	Definition	Example
Jigsaw	A cooperative learning activity in which each student becomes an expert on a small piece of information that is part of a much larger piece.	Teachers arrange students in groups. Each group member is assigned a different piece of information. Group members then join with members of other groups assigned the same piece of information, and research and/or share ideas about the information. Eventually, students return to their original groups to try to "piece together" a clear picture of the topic at hand.
Think-Pair-Share	A cooperative learning activity in which students work together to solve a problem or answer a question about an assigned reading.	**Think** - Teachers begin by asking a specific question about the text. Students "think" about what they know or have learned about the topic. **Pair** - Each student should be paired with another student or a small group. **Share** - Students share their thinking with their partner. Teachers expand the "share" into a whole-class discussion.
Chunking	A reading activity that involves breaking down a difficult text into manageable pieces and having students rewrite these "chunks" in their own words.	A science teacher is working with students on complex science text. Students are overwhelmed by the enormity of the chapter. She has students use a graphic organizer where they write down important phrases and words from each paragraph. Students can then consult the graphic organizer as they move through the text.
Reading Response Journals	A writing activity where students use journals to react to what they read by expressing how they feel and asking questions about the text.	After reading a storybook in class, the teacher asks students to use their reading response journals to respond to the story emotionally, make associations between ideas in the text and their own ideas, and record questions they may have about the story.
Evidence-Based Discussion	The teacher sets the expectation that students use evidence in the text to support claims they make during the discussion.	The class is discussing World War II. Students are split into groups and answer questions on the board. Students must identify where in the text their answer or claim is supported.
Literature Circles	A small-group, cooperative learning activity where students engage and discuss a piece of literature/text.	A teacher divides students into groups. Every student has a role. A teacher distributes an article from the newspaper. Students read the article and then discuss the article. Students engage using their role to understand the text.

Bloom's Taxonomy

This is a hierarchical model used to classify educational learning objectives into levels of complexity and specificity. The higher up the pyramid, the more complex the thinking skills. When answering questions regarding critical thinking, think about Bloom's Taxonomy. Below is an adaptation of Blooms Taxonomy to include more skills. On the ESE exam, you may see some skills that are not in the original Bloom's pyramid. We have modified it here.

> ***Take Note!***
>
> The highest parts of the pyramid are ***apply***, ***create***, ***analyze***, and ***evaluate***. When you are faced with a critical thinking problem on the test, visualize this pyramid, and look for answer choices that support those skills.

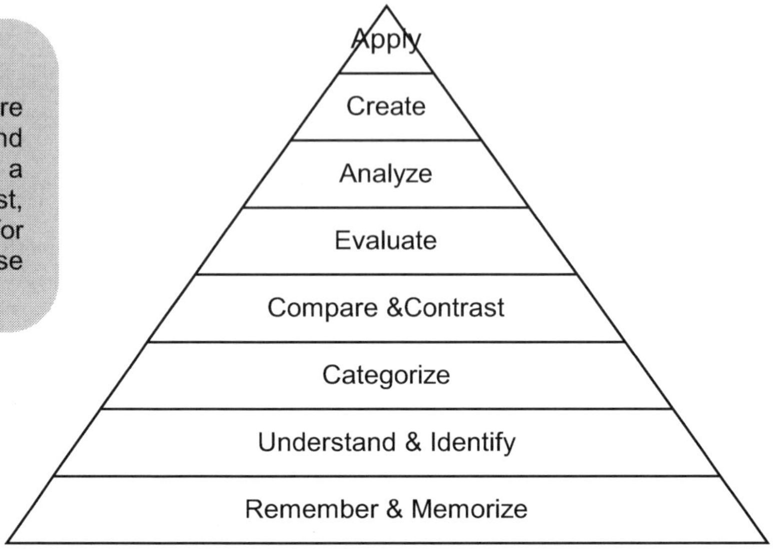

Sample Question

Which of the following would be the most effective activity to increase critical thinking skills in a 3rd grade reading class?

A. Have students work in cooperative groups to identify difficult words in the text.

B. Have students use a graphic organizer to categorize words based on parts of speech.

C. Have students read two different text and evaluate how one text is related to the other.

D. Have students read silently and answer comprehension questions.

> **C** is the only choice with the word *analyze.* Be sure to look for a high-level verb when selecting the correct answer for questions about ***critical thinking.***

Cueing Systems

1. ***Syntactic.*** The syntactic cueing system focuses on the structure of the sentence.
2. ***Semantic.*** The semantic cueing system focuses on the meaning a student derives from text.
3. ***Graphophonic.*** The graphophonic cueing system focuses on the relationship between sounds and symbols, e.g., letter/sound recognition.

> ***Scenario:*** A student writes: ***I no go to park***. This is a syntactic issue. You can understand the meaning, so this is not a semantic issue. The problem is in the structure of the sentence.

Developmental Stages of Writing

Emergent Writing

Writing at this stage means that children begin to understand that writing is a form of communication and their marks on paper convey a message (Mayer, 2007).

- ***Preliterate drawing.*** The student uses drawing to stand for writing and believes that the drawings/writing are communicating a purposeful message.
- ***Preliterate scribbling.*** The student scribbles but intends the scribbles to be writing. The scribbling resembles writing. During this stage, the student holds the pencil correctly.
- ***Emergent.*** The student uses random letters or drawings. Students at this stage also use letter sequences and may write long strings of numbers in random order.
- ***Transitional.*** The student continues to use a variety of different strategies to spell more difficult words. Students at this stage often use inventive spelling.

> ***Scenario:*** A kindergarten student is scribbling in the direction of left to right. The student is in preliterate scribbling.

Fluent Writing

Writing at this stage resembles adult writing. Grammar and spelling are mostly correct, and one can read and understand what the writing says.

Stages of Writing

Preliterate to Emergent	
Scribbling	Random marks or scribbles often occur on a page with drawings. Children may say, "This says Tommy!" (child's name). Toddlers use the terms *drawing* and *writing* to describe their marks; however, three- and four-year olds generally understand the difference between the two.
Emergent	
Mock Handwriting or Wavy Scribble	Children produce lines of wavy scribbles as they imitate adult cursive writing. Children will often pretend they are writing something they have seen their parents write such as a grocery list or letter.
Mock Letters	Children attempt to form alphabetic representations, which also often appear in their drawings. Writing in this stage is often vertical versus horizontal. Children make shapes that resemble conventional letters.
Conventional Letters	Children begin to write letters, usually from their name or a family member's name. As children's mock letters become more and more conventional, real letters of the alphabet begin to appear. Children will often create strings of letters across a page and "read" them as real sentences or a series of sentences.
Invented Spelling (also known as Approximated Spelling)	Children write words using phonemic awareness. The words are not spelled correctly, but do resemble the sounds of the words. For example, invented spelling of the word *was* may be *wuz*, or the invented spelling of the word *other* may be *uther*.
Fluent	
Conventional Spellings	Children's approximated spellings gradually become more and more conventional. The child's own name is usually written first, followed by words such as *mom*, *dad*, and *love*. Initially, children may incorrectly copy words. Eventually, words will be written correctly. Adults can support the child's move to conventional spelling by being patient and by continuing to serve as a good writing model.

Scenario: A kindergarten student is using mock letters to represent words he understands but wants to convey on paper. This student is in the **emergent phase** of writing.

The Writing Process

Learning to write is similar to learning to read. There is a process young learners go through as they become writers of the English language. Like reading, the writing process has several stages:

Prewriting. Brainstorming, considering purpose and goals for writing, using graphic organizers to connect ideas, and designing a coherent structure for a writing piece.

Drafting. Working independently to draft the sentence, essay, or paper.

Peer Review. Students evaluate each other's writing in the peer review process.

Revising. Editing based on structure tone and clear connections.

> ***Quick Tip:*** The peer reviewer reads for content and understanding. The peer reviewer reads through the writing in its entirety and then conferences with his or her partner about suggestions for revision. Then the student revises his or her draft based on that feedback.

Editing. Editing based on conventions and mechanics.

Rewriting. Incorporating changes as they carefully write or type their final drafts.

Publishing. Producing and disseminating the work in a variety of ways, such as a class book, bulletin board, letters to the editor, school newsletter, or website.

Strategies for the Writing Process

Mapping sentences or **diagramming** sentences is when students outline the structure of the sentence, which can help students make sure each piece of the sentence is grammatically correct. It can also give the student a deeper understanding of the English language.

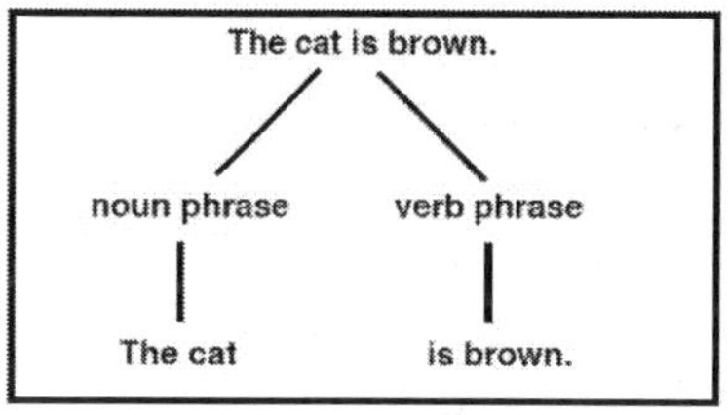

Teachers use **rubrics** to make expectations and grading procedures clear and provide a formative assessment to guide and improve your instruction. Rubrics are then used as a final assessment tool.

Example Rubric

Skill	1 – Minimal	2 – Meets	3 - Exceeds
Mechanics (Syntactic)	Many spelling, grammar, and punctuation errors; sentence fragments; incorrect use of capitalization.	Some spelling and grammar errors; most sentences have punctuation and are complete; uses uppercase and lowercase letters.	Correct spelling, grammar, and punctuation; complete sentences; correct use of capitalization.
Ideas and Content (Semantic)	Key words are not near the beginning; no clear topic; no beginning, middle, and end; ideas are not ordered.	Main idea or topic is in first sentence; semi-defined topic; attempts beginning, middle and end sections; some order of main idea and details in sequence.	Interesting, well-stated main idea or topic sentence; uses logical plan with an effective beginning, middle, and end; good flow of ideas from topic sentence to details in sequence.
Organization	Very unorganized and confusing.	Organized enough to read and understand the ideas.	Very organized and easy to understand.

Modes of Writing

Modes of writing are the variety, conventions, and purposes of the major kinds of language-based communication, particularly writing and speaking.

Four of the most common modes of writing are:

Descriptive. Writing that describes or helps form a visual picture using sensory details and spatial order.

Narrative. A first- person account that tells a story as it happens using sensory details and chronological order.

Expository/Informative Expository. Writing that informs, explains, or tells "how to" without using opinions (just the facts).

Argumentative/Persuasive. Writing that persuades or convinces using support, details, and examples from the text in logical order (most important to least or least important to most). In early grades, this is called *opinion writing*.

> ***Quick Tip:*** Selecting the correct mode for the appropriate occasion and audience is key. Students should understand which mode to use based on what they are trying to say and who they are trying to say it to.

Instructional Methods for Writing

Instructional methods for writing include producing picture books, recipes, brochures, essays, social studies reports, movie reviews, website reviews, letters to the editor, book reviews, and memoirs.

- ***Emphasis on Revision.*** Revising pieces thoughtfully over time, not a new piece of writing each day (much writing will not leave draft form).
- ***Conference/Assessment Notes.*** Keeping a log or portfolio on each student's writing progress.
- ***Spelling and Vocabulary.*** Connecting to both writing, reading and language use.
- ***Sentence Structure and Conventions.*** Practicing in context, using mini-lessons instead of isolated skills sheets.
- ***Meaningful Feedback.*** Providing students with specific details as you review their work.

> ***Quick Tip:*** Communicating expectations is key. Be sure to use rubrics and allow students to use those rubrics before they begin the writing process and as they are writing.

> **Scenario:** After giving a formative assessment, Ms. Jones notices her students are having trouble writing correct sentences. She wants to give them practice so they can write better. She decides to have students map sentences so they can understand the structure. This is considered a **syntactic analysis**.

Evidence-Based Instruction Methods in Math

The following evidence-based methods are designed to increase skills in math across all content areas:

- Modify instruction based on data from formative assessments of students
- Use structured peer-assisted learning activities involving heterogeneous ability groupings
- Use systematic and explicit instruction using visual and graphic representations
- Provide opportunities for students to think aloud while working
- Share and discuss assessment data with students
- Instruction on solving math word problems that are based on common underlying structures including instruction on how to read math problems
- Provide explicit instruction on writing in math such as explaining answers and the processes taken to answer mathematical problems in writing

Progression of Math Knowledge Over Time and Math Fluency

Students evolve as they learn math. Understanding math is just like understanding anything: you start with the concrete and move toward the abstract.

Think C-R-A!

C	R	A
↓	↓	↓
Concrete	**Representation**	**Abstract**
tiling, base ten blocks	pictures, graphics and charts	knowing 2 x 5 is 10.

Math Fluency

- ***Rate.*** How fast can the student solve problems?
- ***Accuracy.*** How many problems did the student solve correctly?
- ***Automaticity.*** Does the student have quick automatic facts memorized? Can the student quickly recite these facts (i.e., multiplication facts)?
- ***Flexibility.*** Can the student solve the problem in different ways?

Competency 6
Knowledge of the Transition Process

1. Determine appropriate programs for career development and career and technical education that meet the needs of individual students with disabilities.
2. Use results of transition assessments to determine appropriate planning strategies to assist the student, parents, caregivers, and stakeholders in developing postsecondary education, career goals, and postschool outcomes.
3. Select instructional approaches to assist students with exceptionalities to engage in self-determination and self-advocacy practices.
4. Identify and compare resources and strategies that can assist individual students with disabilities to function independently in postsecondary education, home and community living, and employment.

Competency 6 makes up 8% of the exam or approximately 10 questions.

Transition Process for ESE Students

According to the Florida Department of Education (2018), ***transition services*** and ***transition planning*** mean to coordinate sets of activities for a student with disabilities that:

- are designed to be within a results-oriented process.
- are focused on improving the academic and functional achievement of the child with a disability to facilitate the child's movement from school to post-school activities, including postsecondary education, vocational education, integrated employment (including supported employment).
- include continuing and adult education, adult services, independent living, or community participation is based on the individual child's needs.
- consider the student's strengths, preferences, and interests, includeing instruction, related services, community experiences, the development of employment and other post-school adult living objectives, and, if appropriate, acquisition of daily living skills and functional vocational evaluation.

Transition Assessments

Transition assessments are the ongoing process of collecting data on individual's needs, preferences, and interests as they relate to the demands of current and future working, living and personal and social environments (The Division on Career Development and Transition of the Council for Exceptional Children, 2018).

- ***Adaptive behavior/daily living skills assessments*** help determine the type and amount of assistance that people with disabilities may need.
- ***Interest inventories*** provide information about an individual's preferences for certain careers, occupational activities, or types of work.
- ***Intelligence tests*** involve a single test or test battery to assess a person's cognitive performance.
- ***Achievement Tests*** measure learning of general or specific academic skills.
- ***Career maturity or employability tests*** are designed to assess developmental stages or tasks on a continuum.
- ***Self-determination assessments*** provide information regarding readiness to make decisions related to their postsecondary ambitions.
- **Transition planning inventories** help identify transition strengths and needs in various aspects of adult living, including employment, postsecondary schooling and training, independent living, interpersonal relationships, and community living.

Job Coaching

Job coaching refers to the training of a student through structured intervention techniques to help learn to perform job tasks and interpersonal skills necessary to be accepted as a worker. A job coach works directly with the student with a disability in training to learn specific requirements of the job such as time and attendance rules and work-related behaviors when dealing with superiors and co-workers.

Self-Determination and Self-Advocacy

Students of all ages should be encouraged to attend and actively participate in their IEP meetings. This is a huge part of self-determination and self-advocacy. Not all students have self-determination and self-advocacy skills. Therefore, students may need instruction and practice in using self-determination and self-advocacy skills, goal-setting strategies, and meeting participation techniques, so they can participate effectively in their IEP process throughout their academic careers.

Self-determination - Self-determination is the ability to identify and achieve goals based on a foundation of *knowing and valuing oneself.* Students must make choices, take control, believe in themselves and act in a manner that helps them achieve in school and career.

The Individuals with Disabilities Act (IDEA) requires that students' preferences and interests be considered and that students be invited to participate in individualized education program (IEP) team meetings when transition services are discussed.

Strategies for building self-determination skills:

- Have students identify other successful people with disabilities.
- Have students discuss their disabilities with people who can help them.
- Have students find out how other people with similar disabilities have been able to get good jobs, go on to college or a vocational program, and live on their own.

Self-advocacy - Self-advocacy is the ability to speak and act on behalf of one's self. Self-advocacy is an important skill ESE students must exercise when attending IEP meetings or deciding how to move forward with their goals.

Self-advocacy skills include:

- being assertive
- knowing one's rights
- negotiating and speaking up for one's self or a cause

Practice Test 1

1. Which of the following shows the least restrictive environment (LRE) to the most restrictive environment?

    A. An ESE student is in a self-contained ESE classroom, an ESE student is participating in culinary class and then goes back to the ESE classroom, an ESE student is in a general education classroom and receives services when needed.

    B. An ESE student is in a self-contained ESE classroom, an ESE student is in a general education classroom and receives services when needed, an ESE student is participating in culinary class and then goes back to the ESE classroom.

    C. An ESE student is participating in culinary class and then goes back to the ESE classroom, an ESE student is in a self-contained ESE classroom, an ESE student is in a general education classroom and receives services when needed.

    D. An ESE student is in a general education classroom and receives services when needed, an ESE student is participating in culinary class and then goes back to the ESE classroom, an ESE student is in a self-contained ESE classroom.

2. Students with disabilities receive at least one annual review of their IEP, are guaranteed due process rights, and are entitled to keeping their records confidential under what federal law?

    A. FAPE

    B. IDEA

    C. LRE

    D. FERPA

3. A copy of procedural safeguards must be provided to the parents/guardians of an exceptional student in all of the following situations EXCEPT:

    A. When a change in placement occurs as a result of a discipline procedure.

    B. When requesting for an evaluation into exceptional student education.

    C. First due process hearing of the school year.

    D. Parent/teacher conference to discuss academics

4. A teacher notices one of her ESE students is not achieving on her math exams. When she looks over the IEP she sees that the goals of the student's IEP is to meet math proficiency at 80%. She determines this goal is too high for the student. She decides to change the goal on the IEP to be more realistic of the student's abilities. What did this teacher fail to consider?

    A. The rights of parents to participate in the decision-making process of the IEP.

    B. The credibility of the IEP team in its ability to make appropriate goals for the student.

    C. The safety of the learning environment.

    D. The quality of instruction.

5. Local public schools must provide services designed to help ESE students meet their annual goals and make progress in the general curriculum at no cost to the parent. This is:

    A. Least Restrictive Environment (LRE)

    B. Procedural Safeguards

    C. Appropriate Evaluation

    D. Free Appropriate Public Education (FAPE)

6. Which of the following is the most common accommodation for ESE students regarding assessments?
   A. peer-assistance
   B. assistive technology
   C. extended time
   D. specialized instruction
7. Attention Deficit and Hyperactivity Disorder (ADHD) is classified under which exceptionality criteria?
   A. Emotional or behavioral disabilities (EBD)
   B. Other Health Impairment (OHI)
   C. Specific learning disabilities (SLD)
   D. Intellectual disabilities (InD)
8. A college student is conducting a case study for a master's program in special education. The college student reaches out to a local ESE teacher for help with the case study. The college student is requesting records of ESE students in the school. What should the ESE teacher do?
   A. Provide the college student with the records after her identity has been verified.
   B. Have the college student call the guidance office to set up an appointment for documentation to be signed before giving out the records.
   C. Have the principal speak with the college student and determine if the records can be given out.
   D. Refuse the college student's request for ESE student records on the grounds of FERPA.
9. Why is there a disproportionate over-representation of English Language Learners (ELLs) in Exceptional Student Education (ESE)?
   A. cultural and language bias
   B. high expectations
   C. low expectations
   D. amount of ELL students in schools
10. An ESE student's parents do not speak or understand English proficiently. What can the school do to make sure the parents are actively involved in the IEP process as protected by IDEA?
    A. Provide all written materials in the parents' native language and require the parents to provide their own translator.
    B. Make a paraprofessional available in the meeting to translate and provide the parents with all the materials in their native language.
    C. Allow the student to translate the meeting and materials to the parents.
    D. Hold the meeting with the parents, allow parents to ask the staffing specialist questions.
11. Which of the following would NOT be included in the IEP?
    A. peer interaction data
    B. classroom accommodations
    C. measurable goals and objectives
    D. least restrictive environment

12. Which of the following would be considered developmentally appropriate characteristics of a 7-year-old student?

   A. Takes turns during playtime, displays self-confidence, seeks constant attention from the teacher.

   B. Raises hand during instruction, works collaboratively during group work, defines long-term academic goals.

   C. Completes short tasks, sits quietly for story time, plays collaboratively on the playground with others.

   D. Displays echolalic behavior, sits quietly during classroom instruction, is aggressive on the playground.

13. A teacher is working on an objective that outlines interpersonal skills. The teacher reads the objective to the class: *use your interpersonal skills to engage with your classmates in a conversation about something that interests you.* The class is then split up, with half the students going with the teacher and the other half going with the paraprofessional assigned to the class. The paraprofessional decides to modify the lesson by having students reread the objective to each other. What is the most appropriate action for the teacher to take?

   A. Tell the principal and ask that the paraprofessional be removed from the classroom.

   B. Ask the students what happened with the paraprofessional.

   C. Ask the paraprofessional to go to another classroom.

   D. Conference with the paraprofessional to make sure she understands she is to follow the teacher's instructions for class.

14. While in an IEP meeting a teacher discovers her student is HIV positive. The teacher is concerned and informs the student's youth soccer coach. Was there anything wrong with what the teacher did?

   A. Yes. The teacher should not have disclosed sensitive and confidential information she learned from the IEP meeting. This is a violation of FERPA.

   B. Yes. The teacher should have put the information in writing as a formal document.

   C. No. The teacher has an obligation to tell the coach because the student is in contact with other students on the soccer field.

   D. No. The teacher is permitted to share confidential information with coaches and other extracurricular personnel.

15. A student's IEP has been finalized in an IEP meeting that was held with all stakeholders. Several weeks later two teachers who were on the team decide the goals of the student should be changed. What should the teachers do to ensure proper protocol?

   A. Change the IEP to meet the needs of the student.

   B. Ask the principal to have the IEP changed.

   C. Call the parents and ask them to change the goal.

   D. Consult with the staffing specialist and schedule a new IEP meeting.

16. Which of the following is an example of an appropriate goal on an IEP?

   A. Within a week, John will stop being hyper in class and listen to the teacher during instruction.

   B. At the end of quarter one, John will increase his math proficiency.

   C. By the end of the year John will independently read a 4th grade reading passage and answer comprehension questions with 80% accuracy.

   D. John will dress appropriately for school.

17. A student with an emotional or behavioral disability is enrolled in a general education classroom and receives consultative services while in the general classroom. The student's behavior issues are escalating and interfering with the student's ability to learn. The IEP team is considering another placement to meet the student's needs. Choose the next least restrictive placement the IEP team would choose for this student.

   A. part-time ESE classroom

   B. full-time ESE classroom

   C. self-contained classroom

   D. special school for behavior problems

18. The IEP team, which includes the student's psychologist, has decided an 8-year-old student should receive services for her emotional disorder. What is the next step the team should take?

   A. Have the parents give the final opinion for what should happen.

   B. Have the principal decide where the student should be placed for accommodations and services.

   C. Determine the least restrictive environment the student will need to function in school.

   D. Ask the student where she prefers to learn.

19. When the IEP team is revising student goals for the year, what should be the most important consideration?

   A. parent desires

   B. teacher desires

   C. student's skills, needs, and interests

   D. other students in the general classroom

20. Which of the following agencies is relevant to educating students with exceptionalities.

   A. Florida Education Finance Committee

   B. Just Read Florida

   C. Florida Healthy Kids

   D. Florida Teachers Union

21. A new ESE teacher has decided to lower the classroom expectations for her ESE students. She believes this will help them achieve at higher rates. The new ESE teacher tells an experienced ESE teacher about her plan. What would be the most appropriate statement the experienced ESE teacher should say to the new ESE teacher?

   A. "Expectations for students should not be lowered. Rather, accommodations should be adhered to, so the student can meet the high expectations every other student is held to."

   B. "Call the parents and ask them if they are ok with the new expectations in the classroom."

   C. "Only lower expectations if the students display extreme disabilities and cannot perform basic tasks."

   D. "Ask the principal if lowering the expectations in your classroom is permitted by the IEP team."

22. A new ESE teacher is eager to attend the IEP meeting of one of her students. The student has been disruptive and difficult to deal with during instruction. The teacher wants the parents to know how ill-behaved the student has been. She is planning to give this feedback to the parents right away. What is wrong with the teacher's plan?

    A. She should present her feedback with detailed data at the beginning of the meeting.

    B. She should solicit other students to communicate what it is like in the classroom when the ESE student misbehaves.

    C. An IEP meeting should start with positive feedback first and move into areas of opportunity to make changes in either behavior or academics.

    D. The teacher should wait for a more experienced ESE teacher to present the behavior data.

23. Which of the following is the most appropriate assistive technology for a student who is classified as visually impaired?

    A. headphones

    B. computer screen reader

    C. voice to text software

    D. interactive whiteboard

24. Which of the following is a funding source for ESE students to attend a private school when the surrounding public schools cannot provide ESE services to the student.

    A. The Florida Lottery Fund

    B. The Federal Private School Fund

    C. The McKay Scholarship

    D. The Charter School Fund

25. An ESE student was involved in an altercation due to an outburst. The principal decides to give the student 10 days out-of-school suspension. The parents disagree with the punishment, citing the student's disability. What is the responsibility of the staffing specialist in this situation?

    A. Hold a manifestation hearing to determine if the altercation was a result of the student's disability.

    B. Refer the parents to the principal and have the principal handle it because it is a discipline issue.

    C. Refer the parents to the student code of conduct, so they can see for themselves what the rules are.

    D. Tell the parents to contact the district if they disagree with the punishment.

26. Which of the following is the correct order of the six steps in the process of planning and delivering ESE services to a student?

    A. Reevaluations, evaluation, eligibility determination, developing the first individual educational plan, consent for services, annual reviews

    B. evaluation, eligibility determination, developing the first individual educational plan, consent for services, annual reviews, reevaluations

    C. annual reviews, evaluation, eligibility determination, developing the first individual educational plan, consent for services, reevaluations

    D. developing the first individual educational plan, evaluation, eligibility determination, consent for services, annual reviews, reevaluations

27. Typical cognitive development for a middle school student would be:

    A. Sensory motor stage

    B. Pre-operational stage

    C. Concrete operational stage

    D. Formal operational stage

28. A formal parent invitation for an IEP meeting must be sent through the US mail within how long until the meeting date?

    A. 3 days

    B. 1 week

    C. 2 weeks

    D. 1 month

29. A fourth-grade teacher notices one of her student's ESE codes changed to hospital homebound (HH). What is expected of this teacher?

    A. Teacher will travel to the student and deliver instruction as if he were in class.

    B. Teacher will need to get a hospital homebound certification to continue to teach the student.

    C. Teacher will put zeroes in for all assignments missed until student returns to class.

    D. Teacher will continue her normal teaching routine with her class and a hospital homebound teacher will be assigned to the student.

30. A teacher creates a timed assessment on multiplication. The quiz is 10 questions in 10 min. Students must complete the quiz with at least 90% accuracy. An ESE student takes the assessment and gets two correct, six incorrect, and two unanswered. What should be the next step in helping the student?

    A. Reteach the material and allow the student to retake the test without being timed.

    B. Assign the same assignment again to the student until he reaches the desired outcome.

    C. Assign extra multiplication homework to remediate the student's skills.

    D. Have a paraprofessional work one-on-one with the student and allow for a retake.

31. Which of the following assessments can be considered as having test bias?

    A. 10 multiple choice questions on a comprehension passage about a boys' baseball team and detailed description about different baseball pitches.

    B. 10 fill-in-the blank questions using new vocabulary from a recent story about the moon.

    C. A short answer test on the scientific method.

    D. An essay on the WWII.

32. After a student submits her test and it is graded by the computer, the teacher sees a raw score of 78. What does this mean?

    A. The student scored 78%.

    B. The student is in the 78th percentile.

    C. The student answered 78 questions correctly.

    D. The student's scale score is 78.

33. An ELL student from another country enrolls in a new school for the first time. The student only speaks Spanish and needs to be tested for ESE. The psychologist speaks Spanish, but in a different dialect than the student speaks. What should the psychologist do?

A. Request a psychologist who speaks the same native language and dialect as the student.

B. Conduct the exam in Spanish and try to make the student understand.

C. Permit the student to enroll only after he can be tested by a private psychologist and supply the results.

D. Direct the student and parent to the district office to allow them to handle the situation.

34. Which of the following would be the most effective way to use a formative assessment?

A. To determine students' percentile ranking.

B. To assess standards on a state test.

C. To diagnose deficits in students' skills.

D. To make instructional decisions.

35. A high school senior, who is also ESE, has taken the Algebra 1 FSA, a graduation requirement. He has not scored the minimum for graduation. He has participated in every retake of the exam. The student has maintained a passing grade in all math classes for all four years. What options does the student have to meet the graduation requirement?

A. Because the student did not pass the FSA, the student is not eligible for graduation.

B. Because the student has maintained a passing score for all four years of math, the IEP team can write a waiver for the student and submit it to the state for approval.

C. Because the student is ESE, he will be granted a special diploma and graduate on time.

D. Because the student is ESE, he can continue to retake the test until he is 21 and graduate within that timeframe.

36. Which of the following would be considered an effective assessment of functional curriculum?

A. A 50-item multiple choice test on US History.

B. An essay assessment for a critical analysis of a poem.

C. A task list on designing and implementing a weekly budget.

D. A formative assessment during a group discussion.

37. A 5th grade ESE teacher has focused a unit on appropriate classroom behavior. What would be the most effective way to assess students' skill management of these skills?

A. Students complete a multiple-choice test on appropriate classroom behavior.

B. A paraprofessional observes students in the classroom and documents their behavior.

C. The teacher documents every time students fail to use the behavior and prescribes consequences.

D. Students document their use of behavior skills across different classroom activities.

38. A teacher examines the cumulative records and IEP of a new ESE student assigned to her class. She discovers that the student is functioning significantly higher in reading and mathematics than the students currently in her classroom. What is the most appropriate first step the teacher should take?

A. Perform a diagnostic assessment to determine the best course of action for the new student.

B. Start the student at the same level as the other students and decide how to move forward.

C. Ask that the student be placed in a different class, since the new student's ability does not match the abilities of those in the classroom.

D. Call the parents and set up a parent teacher conference to discuss suitable alternatives to the student's academic day.

39. A teacher is analyzing a student's behavior after several intervention strategies. What can the teacher determine based on the data presented in the graphs below.

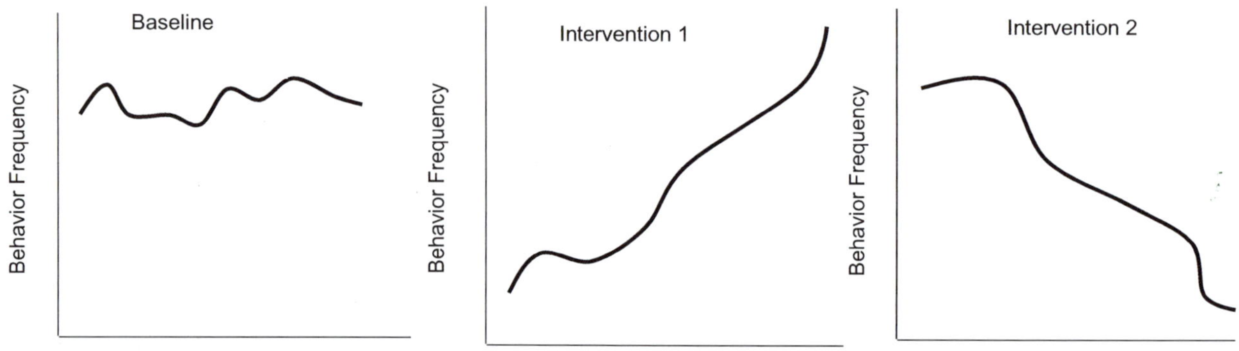

A. A new diagnostic test will need to be administered better baseline data.

B. Intervention 1 is more effective than intervention 2.

C. Intervention 2 is more effective than intervention 1.

D. Neither intervention 1 or intervention 2 was effective.

40. One of the skills outlined in a student's IEP is to actively and appropriately participate in group situations. A teacher has the student actively participate in a cooperative learning exercise. She observes and records the student's efforts in contributing to the group discussion, waiting her turn to speak, and sharing relevant information to the discussion. This assessment is:

A. problem-based.

B. performance-based.

C. project-based.

D. standards-based.

41. A student is given extra time on the state-wide assessment for reading. The student is taking what kind of assessment?

A. norm-referenced

B. diagnostic

C. formative

D. criterion-referenced

42. A severely disabled student, who has limited use of his hands, is taking a math exam in a general education classroom. Which of the following would be appropriate?

A. extended time

B. voice to text writing software with assistance from a paraprofessional.

C. voice to text writing software with assistance from another student.

D. screen reader

43. Which of the following assessments would be most appropriate to use if a teacher wants to assess students' progress in generalizing across settings?

A. a problem-based assessment using language arts skills in social science.

B. a unit exam in science on Florida ecosystems.

C. an informal observation of behavior during reading.

D. a multiple-choice test on state standards in math.

44. Which of the following is an example of a teacher using data to drive instructional decisions in the classroom?

A. A teacher is walking around the room and observing students working on math problems.

B. A teacher conferences with students to discuss feedback of their writing.

C. A teacher uses reading scores to group students temporarily for interventions.

D. A teacher is planning a performance-based assessment.

45. A teacher is using a tally system to document how often and for how long a student displays a certain behavior. What is she assessing?

A. frequency and duration

B. onset and outcome

C. inputs and outputs

D. cause and effect

46. An ESE student is having trouble pronouncing words with the "ch" sound. Which of the following should a teacher consider before applying an intervention to help this student with pronunciation?

A. Is the student ready for interventions?

B. Are the interventions evidence-based?

C. Does the peer teacher approve of the interventions?

D. Is a paraprofessional available to help with the interventions?

47. A middle school teacher is reading over her students' IEPs and determining her instructional approach to a new science unit. What should be the first thing she considers as she plans the lesson?

A. the different exceptionalities in the class

B. the number of students in the class

C. the availability of a paraprofessional

D. the state-adopted academic standards

48. Where is the best place for an ESE teacher to find recent research on effective interventions for ESE students in writing?

   A. online community

   B. ESE association

   C. peer-reviewed academic journal

   D. district curriculum resource room

49. A general education teacher has several ESE students in her classroom. What can she do to make sure all students are learning at the pace and level each student needs?

   A. Differentiate and accommodate students through flexible grouping and accommodations.

   B. Make the curriculum easier for ESE students who are struggling.

   C. Pair ESE students with general education students to diversify classroom activities.

   D. Use a paraprofessional as much as possible to work with the ESE students.

50. Which of the following would be the most appropriate accommodation for an ESE student who struggles to eat with standard utensils because of his cerebral palsy?

   A. Have a paraprofessional feed the student during lunch.

   B. Encourage the student to use a special spoon with a large grip.

   C. Put the student in a separate room so he can use his hands to eat.

   D. Have the student use a standard spoon instead a standard fork.

51. A third-grade student is displaying difficulty in literacy, specifically multi-syllable words. The teacher has implemented evidence-based interventions and nothing seems to help the student. She suspects the student may have a learning disability. What would be the most effective next step for the teacher to take in this situation?

   A. Ask the guidance counselor to call the parents and tell them he probably needs an IEP.

   B. Call an ESE meeting and invite the parents to listen to suggestions regarding classifying the student as ESE.

   C. Begin the process of implementing a multi-tiered system of supports (MTSS) for the student.

   D. Call the parents and ask that they have the student independently tested for a reading disability.

52. An ESE student is having a hard time focusing during reading time in class. He often acts out during this time in class. What is the most effective strategy the teacher can use when the student acts out?

   A. Ignore the student's bad behavior, focus on the students who are behaving appropriately, and reward positive behavior happening in the room.

   B. Ask the student to leave the classroom so the other students are not affected.

   C. Have the paraprofessional take the student out into the hall until the reading portion of class is over.

   D. Threaten to call the student's parents because that has worked in the past.

53. Which of the following is the most effective way to integrate language arts into other disciplines in the class?

   A. Have students write essays at the end of each lesson.

   B. Have students identify areas in the lesson where language arts apply.

   C. Have students pair up and discuss language arts strategies they enjoy using in class.

   D. Have students apply language arts skills, when appropriate, during lessons in different content areas.

54. Which of the following is an example of functional curriculum?

   A. Students are writing essays about real-world situations.

   B. Students are completing a task list for opening a checking account.

   C. Students are listening to a guest speaker about working at the airport.

   D. Students are working in cooperative groups to analyze literature.

55. Identify the most appropriate rationale for using a task analysis in a mathematics class.

   A. Students can learn complex concepts.

   B. Students can work cooperatively.

   C. Students can stay on track regardless of skill.

   D. Students can display mastery based on their individual needs.

56. A student is having difficulty pronouncing the correct sounds in words. The student is struggling with:

   A. phonemes

   B. phonics

   C. sight words

   D. syllables

57. An ESE paraprofessional informs a teacher that she only wants to assist certain ESE students whom she feels comfortable with. What should the teacher tell the paraprofessional?

   A. "I need the opportunity to work with all students. Therefore, you will need to work with different groups of students in accordance to what students need throughout the day."

   B. "Please find another classroom to be a paraprofessional in. I need to find someone who can work with all students."

   C. "I will be informing the principal that you are not doing your job."

   D. "I want you to feel comfortable, so we will find a way for you to only work with the students you feel comfortable with."

58. Two ESE students are being disruptive during a history lesson in a 10th grade class. What would be the most appropriate way to address the behavior?

   A. Write the students up and tell them to go to the office.

   B. Ask the students to act appropriately during the lesson.

   C. Continue with the lesson, walk over to the two students, and use proximity control.

   D. Tell the students you will be calling their parents.

59. Which of the following is an example of a Tier 3 level of MTSS?

   A. Students are receiving direct instruction on a science unit.

   B. Students are participating in flexible grouping to meet their needs.

   C. Students are pulled out of the class for intensive instruction in speech.

   D. Students are working in cooperative groups to solve math problems.

60. Which of the following is an example of anecdotal observation notes?

A. The student is behaving in class.

B. The student is sitting quietly before the lesson begins.

C. The student has difficulty in phonics instruction.

D. The student has increased positive behavior by 20%.

61. An ESE teacher becomes aware that another general education teacher is not using the strategies outlined in a student's IEP. Which of the following approaches should the ESE teacher take in addressing this situation?

A. Tell the principal that the general education teacher is not following the IEP.

B. Call an IEP meeting and inform the parents that the student is not receiving the proper accommodations during general education classes.

C. Write a formal complaint to the district.

D. Remind the teacher that the IEP and the accommodations outlined in the IEP should be followed and offer support for the teacher if she is having trouble implementing them.

62. A student has a short-term memory disability. Which of the following accommodations would be the most appropriate for this student whose exceptionality is specific learning disability (SLD)?

A. Provide large-font print of the test.

B. Allow the student to use a computer screen reader.

C. Seat the student in the front of the room.

D. Allow the student to use his notes during classroom exams.

63. A teacher is creating lesson plans for the quarter. She is using one of her favorite blogs to guide her planning of lessons for ESE students. What is wrong with this method?

A. She needs to make sure the person writing the blog is a teacher.

B. She should use research-based strategies and methods when planning lessons.

C. She should ask her department head if the blog is appropriate.

D. There is nothing wrong with this method because people use blogs all the time in education.

64. Which of the following would be most appropriate for a student who struggles with reading comprehension?

A. metacognition strategies

B. extended time

C. audio books

D. repeated reading

65. A teacher is taking students out of their general education classroom to administer intensive reading and writing strategies. What is this called?

A. substitute teaching method

B. push-in teaching method

C. pull-out teaching method

D. isolation teaching method

66. A teacher with a severely disabled student in the class wants to administer a lesson on how to make a sandwich. What should be established beforehand with the student, so the lesson is effective?

A. Perform a task analysis.

B. Perform a diagnostic analysis.

C. Perform a behavior analysis.

D. Perform a safety analysis.

67. Which of the following is an example of cross-curricular application strategies?

A. Students are writing an essay about WWII.

B. Students are using math applications in a science unit.

C. Students are reading and writing in science class.

D. Students use the internet to research various topics in math and science.

68. Which of the following should a teacher consider first when she is working on accommodations for a student with a short-term processing disorder.

A. how the general education students in the class will react

B. what the parents want for the student

C. the state-adopted academic standards

D. the equipment needed to accommodate the student.

69. On a recent reading assessment, an ESE student scores below grade-level. What would be the most appropriate instructional method the teacher can use?

A. Group the student with other students who achieve at low levels.

B. Request a paraprofessional to work with the student full-time.

C. Use differentiated instruction along with supplemental materials to accommodate for the student.

D. Request the IEP team discuss necessary modifications for the student.

70. Which of the following would be considered tier 1 interventions?

A. Interventions some of the students receive in a general education class.

B. Interventions only one student receives in a general education class.

C. Interventions none of the students receive in a general education class.

D. Interventions all of the students receive in a general education class.

71. A 10th grade ESE student is acting out in class. She uses profanity and is combative with the teacher. The teacher writes a referral and asks that the student be suspended from school. What must the assistant principal do first before she can suspend the student?

A. Determine if the student's behavior is a manifestation of her disability.

B. Call the parents and ask them to attend a behavior meeting.

C. Interview the teacher and be sure she followed the IEP behavior plan.

D. Interview the student and get her side of the story.

72. Which of the following anecdotal evidence is most effective when analyzing student behavior?

   A. The student does not pay attention during class.

   B. The student disrupts the teacher during lessons.

   C. The student throws paper and calls out during instruction.

   D. The student seems angry and agitated in class.

73. A teacher is having a hard time getting students to settle down during cooperative learning. The students are disruptive and unfocused. She decides to tell the students if they can work quietly in groups and get all their work done for the next 3 days, they will receive an ice cream party at the end of the week. What tactic did the teacher use?

   A. extrinsic rewards and group contingency

   B. intrinsic rewards and individual accountability

   C. intrinsic rewards and group contingency

   D. extrinsic rewards individual accountability

74. Ms. Jones uses a tally system to record the occurrence of a target behavior when she implements a behavior intervention system for her ESE student. This will help the teacher to:

   A. understand the student more accurately.

   B. count the number of times the student used desired behavior.

   C. define the number of times a student used desired behavior.

   D. diagnose the student's behavior.

75. Which of the following is an example of positive behavior support?

   A. A teacher writes a student up every time he calls out in class.

   B. A teacher pairs students together who will be a positive influence on each other.

   C. A teacher rewards positive behavior and ignores negative behavior.

   D. A teacher calls the parents of a student and asks for support at home.

76. A student is having difficulty working with peers during cooperative learning. He often calls out and uses profanity during group work. The student and the teacher develop a plan calling for the student to be rewarded when the student controls his behavior and for the student to receive consequences when he does not control his behavior. This strategy is an example of:

   A. planned ignoring

   B. positive consequences

   C. negative practice

   D. contingency contracting

77. A teacher is having a hard time with an ESE student during reading time in class. The teacher wants to address the behavior in an effective way. What should she do first?

   A. Call the student's parents and ask for support at home.

   B. Set aside time to observe the behavior while it is happening.

   C. Ask the assistant principal for help.

   D. Have the paraprofessional tally how many times the student acts out during instruction.

78. This is a set of research-based strategies used to increase quality of life and decrease problem behavior by teaching new skills and making changes in a person's environment.

A. intervention supports

B. multi-tiered system of supports

C. environmental behavior support.

D. positive behavior support

79. A teacher who has several ESE students with behavioral exceptionalities wants to implement a functional behavior assessment. Which of the following steps should she take?

A. define the problem behavior, collect behavioral data, analyze the behavioral data, develop a behavior intervention plan, progress monitor the plan.

B. define the problem behavior, call an IEP meeting to ask for assistance, develop a behavior intervention plan, progress monitor the plan.

C. define the problem behavior, collect behavioral data, prescribe consequences for bad behaviors, keep parents informed of student progress.

D. define the problem behavior, have the paraprofessional collect behavioral data, analyze the behavioral data, present the data to the next IEP meeting.

80. A teacher is using intervention strategies for an ESE student who has trouble interacting appropriately with other students during playtime. What should the teacher do first when helping students manage their behavior?

A. Call the parents and let them know of the plan for the students.

B. Display rules on the board for students to follow.

C. Set clear expectations for students.

D. Use consequences for behavior when it happens.

81. A 3rd grade ESE student is struggling walking in a line to the lunch room. She repeatedly jumps out of line and runs in front of the teacher towards the lunch room. The teacher has tried incentives, contingencies and phone calls home. What would be an effective strategy for the teacher to use in this situation.

A. Require the student to sign a behavior contract that outlines consequences for disruptive behavior.

B. Design a behavior contract with the student that outlines positive behavior and strategies to achieve positive behavior.

C. Request that the student be put in a full-time ESE self-contained classroom, so her behavior can be monitored and corrected.

D. Ask that the principal walk the class to the lunch room because the student behaves when the principal is around.

82. Ms. Miller is working with an ESE student who has trouble acting appropriately in class. Which of the following is most effective when getting students to act appropriately in class?

A. Have the principal come in and talk to the class about good behavior.

B. Encourage students to read stories about good behavior in class.

C. Implement a tally system to regulate student behavior in class.

D. Model appropriate behavior and specifically praise students when they act appropriately.

83. A teacher is trying to get her students to settle down after lunch and prepare for the next lesson. Which of the following would be the most effective way to communicate to students that she would like them to settle down and start the lesson?

A. "Please sit down and stop talking. We will begin then lesson when everyone is behaving appropriately."

B. "Jose, I love how you came in quietly, got your book and prepared to start the lesson. You too Jocelyn. Thank you so much!"

C. "We will not have recess today if you all cannot settle down. We have work to do, and if we do not get to it, there will be no playtime."

D. "I have some candy and cookies for students who can come in, sit down, and prepare for the lesson."

84. Which of the following is considered an intrinsic reward for positive behavior?

A. receiving praise for sitting quietly

B. gaining extra points for positive behavior

C. extra time on the playground for sharing

D. feeling confident after behaving appropriately

85. An ESE student who is also autistic is repeating words and phrases. The student is displaying signs of:

A. echolalia

B. babbling

C. cooing

D. modulation

86. A teacher has several students who have reached the highest level of language development. These students are applying the rules of language in different context. These students' level is:

A. pre-alphabetic

B. partial alphabetic

C. pragmatic

D. syntax

87. A first grade ESE student is breaking down the word cat like this C-A-T. What strategy is the student using?

A. phonic segmentation

B. semantic segmentation

C. pre-alphabetic segmentation

D. phonemic segmentation

88. Students are looking at the list of words below. What would be the best strategy to use with these words?

incredible, credibility, and credit

A. phonics

B. phonemic awareness

C. etymology

D. sight word analysis

89. An ESE teacher is going over word structure in this order: cvc. cvcc, cvcv, ccvcc. What method is she using?

A. systematic word arrangement

B. semantic word arrangement

C. comprehensive word arrangement

D. metacognitive word arrangement

90. A teacher is walking around the room, reading from her book, and showing students her process for working through difficult words. The teacher is using a technique called:

A. decoding.

B. structural analysis.

C. modeling.

D. semantic mapping.

91. A teacher is helping her students study word forms and word relationships. She and the students are analyzing the structure of words and parts of words, such as stems, root words, prefixes, and suffixes. The teacher is working with students on:

A. phonemic awareness

B. phonological awareness

C. semantic analysis

D. morphology

92. When a student has awareness of phonemes in words, syllables, onset-rime segments, and spelling, he or she is demonstrating:

A. phonological awareness.

B. phonics mastery.

C. phonemic awareness.

D. structural analysis.

93. An ESE teacher is working with students using semantic analysis. What type of questions should she be asking the students?

A. "Are the words in the story spelled correctly?"

B. "What does it mean when the character talks to his father?"

C. "How many characters are there in the story?

D. "What are the key words used in the story?"

94. Phonemic awareness includes the ability to:

A. form compound words and combine word parts.

B. spell accurately and decode unfamiliar words.

C. pronounce individual sounds in words.

D. differentiate between homonyms and spell accurately.

95. Metacognition is an important skill students need to comprehend text. What activity would be best to foster metacognition in students?

A. round robin reading

B. read aloud/think aloud

C. silent sustained reading

D. popcorn reading

96. An ESE teacher wants to increase comprehension and critical thinking in her 3rd grade students. What would be the most effective strategy to use?

A. Have students work in cooperative learning groups to identify difficult words.

B. Have students engage in paired reading to understand tone.

C. Have students work individually to categorize complex vocab words.

D. Have students work individually to evaluate text structure and meaning.

97. A third grade ESE student who struggles with comprehension has a goal in his IEP to be able to explain a series of events in a story. What would be an appropriate way for the teacher to use an authentic assessment to measure his comprehension?

A. Take a multiple-choice test.

B. Draw a picture representing the story.

C. Write a paragraph about the story.

D. Identify vocab words used in the story.

98. Which of the following strategies is most effective in increasing students' automaticity and fluency.

A. repeated reading

B. read aloud think aloud

C. structural analysis

D. phonological awareness

99. Which of the following is effective in building fluency and confidence?

A. choral reading

B. popcorn reading

C. round robin reading

D. literature circles

100. Trina is a fifth-grade ESE student who can read words by remembering visual or contextual cues. She recognizes and reads signs and labels in her school and home environments but cannot read these words when they are shown in isolation. She also lacks the ability to match letters to sounds. What phase of word recognition is Trina demonstrating?

A. full-alphabetic

B. pre-alphabetic

C. partial-alphabetic

D. consolidated-alphabetic

101. Jose has a goal on his IEP to increase his reading ability to the independent level for grade level books. At what percentage accuracy should he be reading to be considered at the independent level?

A. 80%-85%

B. 85%-90%

C. 90%-95%

D. 95%-100%

102. Students are breaking down words using prefixes and suffixes. They are conducting a:

A. structural analysis.

B. semantic analysis.

C. phonics analysis.

D. rubric analysis.

103. A 4th grade ESE teacher is showing students how to read from left to right. She is focusing on:

A. phonemic awareness.

B. phonics.

C. directionality.

D. semantic analysis.

104. Ms. Johnson can tell her gifted student, Amanda, finishes her work early and is usually bored. What can Ms. Johnson do to ensure Amanda is receiving a challenging and fulfilling education?

A. Provide her with more homework and rewards for completing it.

B. Have Amanda help other students who need assistance.

C. Conference with Amanda and map a plan together on how to increase rigor.

D. Have Amanda complete her assignments and then read a book of her choice.

105. A 10th grade general education teacher is working with her ESE students on writing. If the teacher wants to clearly convey expectations and feedback she should provide students with a:

A. rubric before writing assignments.

B. rubric before and during writing assignments.

C. rubric after writing assignments.

D. rubric before, during, and after writing assignments.

106. A 3rd grade ESE teacher is working with students on text-to-text connection. Students should be:

A. relating the text to life experiences.

B. relating text to another text he or she read before.

C. connecting one topic of a book to an interdisciplinary unit.

D. connecting one book to a story from his or her past.

107. Students are in groups reading and analyzing text. Each student in the group is accountable for a job. Two students are readers, another is a note taker, and another is the administrator. What type of cooperative learning structure are the students engaging in?

A. think-pair-share

B. literature circles

C. read aloud/think aloud

D. guided reading

108. A paraprofessional is working in small groups with her ESE students. She is reading from her book and showing students her process for working through difficult words. The teacher is using a technique called:

A. decoding.

B. structural analysis.

C. read aloud/think aloud.

D. semantic mapping.

109. What is the most effective way to teach new vocabulary to students?

A. Study new words in context.

B. Write new words and their definitions.

C. Write a story using new words.

D. Study new words for homework.

110. Which of the following would be the most effective tool to help a 5th grade ESE student convey her feeling about a story?

A. reading response journals

B. multiple choice test

C. formative assessment

D. cooperative learning

111. Students are receiving guidance on how to fill out employment applications. They are also making lists of things they need from the grocery store. These students are working on:

A. basic skills remediation.

B. work-study curriculum

C. reading curriculum

D. functional curriculum

112. A 12th grade student has been working through a community-based ESE program, where she works at a local grocery store since she was 16 years old. Upon completion of the school year, her boss has agreed to keep her on the job while she receives additional training. This model is called

A. sheltered employment

B. job shadowing

C. support employment

D. career education

113. A student is telling her IEP team that she is ready to revise her goals in reading. She wants to focus on comprehension and critical thinking. This student is exercising:

A. self-advocacy

B. self-determination

C. self-respect

D. self-confidence

114. Students in a life-skills class are taking an assessment to determine what type of job they may want or be suited for after high school. What type of transition assessment are the students taking?

A. adaptive behavior/daily living skills assessments

B. achievement tests

C. interest inventories

D. state standardized tests

115. When an ESE student turns 16, the student and the IEP team will begin the process of developing a(n)

A. transitional IEP

B. adaptive IEP

C. goal-centered IEP

D. traditional IEP

116. An employer of an ESE student calls the ESE staffing specialist and says the student is not behaving properly at work and is having outbursts. What should the staffing specialist do?

A. Tell the manager the student will be put on probation.

B. Have the manager call the student and the student's parents directly about the situation.

C. Have the student apologize to the manager and rectify the behavior.

D. Work with the manager and the student to implement the behavior intervention plan at the workplace.

117. A teacher has refused to give an ESE student her accommodations because the teacher says she doesn't have time. A student knows she should be receiving her accommodations. She tells the teacher she wants her assistive technology and her accommodations as outlined in her IEP. The student is exercising:

A. self-advocacy

B. self-determination

C. self-respect

D. self-confidence

118. Which of the following is used to focus on improving the academic and functional achievement of the child with a disability to facilitate the child's movement from school to post-school activities, including postsecondary education, vocational education, or integrated employment?

A. transition planning

B. interdisciplinary curriculum

C. adaptive services

D. paraprofessionals

119. Which of the following should be most important when designing and implementing a transitional IEP?

A. student interdependence

B. student reliance

C. student self-esteem

D. student independence

120. Which of the following is appropriate for a 22-year-old to learn job skills?

A. technical school

B. apprenticeship program

C. post-secondary institution

D. GED program

#	Answer	Comp	Explanation
1.	D	1	Children with disabilities have the right to receive their education in the school and the classroom they would attend if they were not disabled. However, some students need special classes or services. The goal is to keep ESE students included in the general curriculum. The least restrictive environment in this item is general classroom. The second is participating in culinary and then going back into an ESE classroom. And the most restrictive environment here is the self-contained classroom.
2.	B	1	IDEA is the Individuals with Disabilities Education Act and is a Federal law enacted in 1975. FAPE is Free and Appropriate Public Education, LRE is Least Restrictive Environment, and FERPA is Family Educational Rights and Privacy Act.
3.	D	1	Procedural safeguards are rules and procedures that must be used when making decisions about a student's ESE services. A parent teacher conference on academics does not apply.
4.	A	1	Parents and students have the right, under the law, to be actively involved with the IEP process and decisions made by the IEP team. A teacher should NEVER make changes to an IEP. Rather, she should share observations and data during the IEP meeting, so the team can make decisions collectively. The team includes the parents and the student.
5.	D	1	Under Free Appropriate Public Education (FAPE), students who live in Florida, who are at least three years old and less than 22 years old, who meet the eligibility criteria, and who have not yet graduated from high school with a standard diploma, are entitled to receive free exceptional education services from the local school district.
6.	C	1	Extended time is a very common accommodation for ESE students regarding classroom assessments and state standardized assessments.
7.	B	1	According to the Florida Department of Education (2018), other health impairment (OHI) means having limited strength, vitality or alertness, including a heightened alertness to environmental stimuli, that results in limited alertness with respect to the educational environment, that is due to chronic or acute health problems. This includes, but is not limited to, asthma, attention deficit disorder or attention deficit hyperactivity disorder, Tourette syndrome, diabetes, epilepsy, a heart condition, hemophilia, lead poisoning, leukemia, nephritis, rheumatic fever, sickle cell anemia, and acquired brain injury.
8.	D	1	Never give out information regarding any student, but especially ESE students. ESE students' confidential records are protected under FERPA and under IDEA. When in doubt, DON'T give it out.

#	Answer	Comp	Explanation
9.	A	1	Too often, students who struggle with the language are labeled with learning disabilities. This is considered cultural or language bias because language and culture was not considered when classifying these students as ESE. Just because someone is not proficient in English, does not mean he or she has a learning disability.
10.	B	1	Parents should be actively involved in the IEP process and need to understand everything going on the IEP meeting. If parents do not speak English, the school must provide proper accommodations so the parents can understand what is happening in the meetings. This is the right of the parents, which is protected under the federal law, IDEA.
11.	A	1	Be on the lookout for nonsense. Peer interaction data is not a thing. In addition, accommodations, goals/objectives, and least restrictive environment are all part of the IEP.
12.	C	1	Be on the lookout for these "list" answer choices. The key words in the question are *developmentally appropriate.* A and D have negative behaviors: seek constant attention and aggressive on the playground. Also, echolalic behavior is repetition of words or sounds occurring in people who are on the autistic spectrum. B is not the correct choice because defining long-term academic goals is not something a 7-year-old does. Therefore, C is the best answer here.
13.	D	1	Special education paraprofessionals assist students with special needs under the direction of a certified teacher.
14.	A	1	When in doubt, don't give it out. This is an example of a teacher violating the student's rights as defined under IDEA, FERPA and HIPPA.
15.	D	1	Goals can only be modified during an IEP meeting with all stakeholders involved. Teachers cannot change goals as they see fit. Therefore, scheduling a new IEP meeting is the best course of action here.
16.	C	1	IEP goals should be SMART: specific, measurable, achievable, relevant and timely. Answer choices A and D are too general to be an appropriate goal and do not follow the SMART criteria. While answer choice B is a goal, increasing proficiency is not specific enough to be SMART. Therefore, C is the best answer here.
17.	A	1	The next LRE here is part-time ESE classroom. Full-time ESE, self-contained ESE classroom, and a special school for behavioral problems are the most restrictive here. A is the best choice for LRE.
18.	C	1	If you see the term least restrictive environment in the answer choices, it is probably the correct answer. One of the goals of the IEP team should be to keep the ESE student in as many general education classes as possible. Sometimes students need full-time

#	Answer	Comp	Explanation
			ESE classrooms or self-contained classrooms. However, that is only if their learning is negatively affected by the general classroom environment.
19.	C	1	The most important things to consider when revising goals are the skills and abilities of the student. The student's interests should also be taken into consideration. Parent and teacher desires are not always in line with what is best for the ESE student. Finally, other students in the classroom should not be a main consideration of the IEP team. The team is there for the ESE student, and the ESE student should be the focus.
20.	C	1	Florida Healthy Kids deals with the health of students. Therefore, it is your best answer here. Remember, go with the obvious, or at least the most likely choice.
21.	A	1	Never, EVER, lower expectations for students. Instead, teachers must scaffold and accommodate so ESE students can meet the expectations all students are held to.
22.	C	1	Teachers should never start an IEP meeting with negative feedback. These meetings are to help the student achieve. Therefore, positive feedback should be the focus. Misbehavior can be addressed in the meeting, and the team can reevaluate the goals to mitigate the bad behavior. Always be positive first.
23.	B	1	If the student is visually impaired, he or she may not be able to read the computer screen during computer time. Therefore, a screen reader is most appropriate here. None of the other assistive technologies are appropriate for this student's exceptionality.
24.	C	1	The McKay Scholarship Fund provides funds for ESE students to attend private school if those private schools can provide better accommodations or services than the public schools can provide.
25.	A	1	Before an ESE student can receive severe punishment, such as out of school suspension, for a behavior, a staffing specialist must hold a manifestation hearing to determine that the behavior was not part of the exceptionality of the student. Only when the behavior is deemed unrelated to the student's disability can the student be suspended.
26.	B	1	Evaluation has to be first. The team cannot conduct reevaluations, conduct annual reviews or develop an initial IEP until the student is evaluated. Therefore, B is the correct answer here.
27.	C	1	According to Piaget's cognitive development model, students from ages 7-12 (middle school age) should be in the concrete operational stage. Students at this age display logical reasoning about concrete objects. They engage in conservation, reversibility, serial ordering, and understanding cause and effect relationships

#	Answer	Comp	Explanation
			are hallmarks of this stage, but thinking is still limited to the concrete.
28.	C	1	By law, the parents of an ESE student must be notified within 2 weeks, so they can plan accordingly. Some parents may need to take off work or arrange for childcare.
29.	D	1	Once a child is hospital homebound, a specialized teacher, who is often based at the district office, will serve the hospital homebound student. The hospital homebound teacher travels to the students who are classified HH.
30.	A	2	The most common accommodation in ESE is extra time. To see what the student really knows, the teacher can extend the time and allow the student to focus on accuracy, rather than speed.
31.	A	2	Because the passage the students are tested on focuses mainly on gender specific elements, this can be considered test bias. The other three answer choices are general enough to be as objective as possible.
32.	C	2	A raw score is one that measures how many correct items a student scored on the exam.
33.	A	2	When testing students for ESE, one must be able to convey the test directions and content so the student understands. If the student is limited because of language, the person testing the student cannot really determine what the student can or cannot do. Therefore, every effort must be made to administer assessments in the student's home language.
34.	D	2	Using assessments to make instructional decisions is probably the correct answer every time you see it in an answer choice. The state wants to ensure that you will use data to make decisions in the classroom. Formative assessments are a great way to gather important data and make instructional decisions based on that data.
35.	B	2	The IEP team can submit a waiver to the state to waive testing requirements. The ESE student will still graduate as long as the ESE student participates in retakes, maintains a 2.0 GPA in the subject area, and earns the required minimum graduation credits.
36.	C	2	Functional curriculum is one that emphasizes real-world tasks. In this case C is the most functional task of all 4 answers.
37.	D	2	Skill maintenance is about using appropriate skills across different real-world tasks. In addition, students should be taking ownership of these behaviors. When students document their use of the skills in context, they are able to take ownership of their learning and connect the skills to real-life. Remember, stay away from negative answers like C. A multiple choice test will not help students maintain skill

#	Answer	Comp	Explanation
			management. Bringing an outside person, like the paraprofessional in B, is not appropriate.
38.	A	2	This is a differentiation question. Teachers must differentiate instruction based on the student's needs. Before deciding on how to differentiate for this student, the teacher needs data. The only answer choice that provides data is B and C—diagnostic test data. Answer choice B is the opposite of differentiation. Calling the parents—answer choice D—is ineffective at this point.
39.	C	2	In this case, the frequency of behavior goes up with intervention 1. The frequency of behavior goes down with intervention 2. Therefore, intervention 2 is more effective than intervention 1.
40.	B	2	A performance-based assessment measures a student's ability to apply knowledge or skills to perform a task in a relevant situation. In this case, the student is using appropriate behavior in a group setting. Answer choice **B** is the best answer here.
41.	D	2	Criterion-reference tests assess the student's mastery of the state standards. Norm-referenced assessments compare percentile ranking among students. A formative assessment is an ongoing informal assessment a teacher uses to make daily decisions in the classroom. A diagnostic assessment is used to diagnose any problems students are having in learning.
42.	B	2	In this case, the student needs assistance with writing. Therefore, voice to text software is most appropriate. In addition, having a paraprofessional assist is also most appropriate. Never use students as paraprofessionals or tutors. Students are there to learn, not do the work the paraprofessionals and teachers should do.
43.	A	2	The key words here are *generalizing across settings*. This means students are using their skills and understanding in one area and applying it to another area. Therefore, A is the best choice here.
44.	C	2	In every answer choice the teacher is administering an assessment of some kind. However, only in answer choice C does she make a decision—grouping and interventions.
45.	A	2	Frequency refers to how often something happens, and duration refers to how long something happens.
46.	B	3	Remember, if you see the words *evidence-based* or *research-based,* it is most likely the correct answer. All interventions used with students should have evidence or research to support their use. There should be evidence that the interventions work.
47.	D	3	Always start with the standards. If standards are in the answer choice, it's the correct answer. The state writes this test. The state wants to know that you will follow the standards.

#	Answer	Comp	Explanation
48.	C	3	Peer-reviewed academic journals in a database, like EBSCO or ProQuest is the most reliable place to find academic research. The other answer choices are ok. However, a peer-reviewed journal is where teachers can find evidence-based practices.
49.	A	3	*Differentiation* and *accommodation* are good words to be on the lookout for in terms of correct answers. B is never the answer because teachers should NEVER make the curriculum easier for any students. Instead, the expectations should stay high, and the teacher should use differentiation and accommodations to help students achieve. Pairing ESE students with general education students is ok but usually not the answer on these exams. And only using a paraprofessional for ESE kids is not the answer. The para is there for support not to be the only one working with ESE students.
50.	B	3	The goal for any ESE student, regardless of the severity of the disability, is to assimilate or participate in everyday activities. This includes eating. The ESE student should be encouraged to eat independently but with accommodations.
51.	C	3	MTSS is a way to support students before the student is classified as ESE. ESE classification can be permanent; before that happens, the teacher must intervene first. The MTSS process can often help a student get through difficult situations without being classified ESE.
52.	A	3	The most effective strategy here is to ignore negative behavior and reward positive behavior. The other 3 answer choices are punitive, and anything punitive is usually not the correct answer.
53.	D	3	In this case, the application of the skill is best. Simply writing essays at the end of each lesson is not an effective way to integrate language arts. Identifying and discussing areas where language arts can be used is not enough. Answer choice D has the word apply in it. Authentic application is key when integrating language arts in other content areas.
54.	B	3	Functional curriculum requires students to apply skills in the real world. In this case, opening a checking account and completing a task list is the most real-world application out of all the answer choices.
55.	D	3	The phrase *individual needs* is code for differentiation. Anytime you can choose *differentiation* on this exam, choose it.
56.	A	3	Phonemes are the individual sounds in words. Phonics is spelling.
57.	A	3	Answer choice A is the correct answer because it is the most diplomatic out of the 4 and it addresses the problem head on.
58.	C	4	Proximity control is a way to address bad behavior without stopping the lesson. The teacher simply continues with the lesson, so the other students do not miss out on learning. While the teacher

#	Answer	Comp	Explanation
			continues the lesson, she simply walks over to the students and makes her presence known.
59.	C	3	Tier 3 interventions are what only some students, who need the most help, receive. In this case, pulling students out of the classroom to receive intensive interventions is tier 3.
60.	B	3	Anecdotal notes are specific regarding observations in class. Answer choice B addresses the specific behaviors happening. Answer choice A and C are too general to be anecdotal. Answer choice D just gives a percentage. An anecdote is a story. Therefore, look for the story in this situation and B is the answer.
61.	D	3	Reminding the teacher and offering support is the best approach here. Telling the principal, calling an IEP meeting, or informing the district is drastic. Approaching the teacher first and offering support is the best first step. If the teacher continues to ignore the IEP, informing the IEP team or principal would be appropriate.
62.	D	3	Because the student's exceptionality is short-term memory loss, he will need his notes to remember concepts. A screen reader and large font (answer choices A and B) are for visually impaired students. Seating the student in the front of the room is not going to help with memory loss.
63.	B	3	Of course, teachers look at blogs, Pinterest, social media and more to help them with ideas for lessons. However, research-based methods are key. Also, if you see the words research-based or evidence-based in the answer choices, it is definitely your answer.
64.	A	3	Metacognition is classified as thinking about thinking. This means that students learn how their brain works during activities like reading. This is helpful when teaching comprehension.
65.	C	3	The teacher is pulling students out of the classroom. Therefore, the best answer is C.
66.	A	3	A task analysis is used to determine if the student is able to perform a task. In this case, the task is making a sandwich. The teacher would need to determine if the student can use her hands in order for the task to be completed.
67.	B	3	When students apply the skills in one content area to another content area, that is cross-curricular activities. A, C and D are too general. Of course, students read and write in these classes. However, applying knowledge from one content area to a specific part of another content area is key.
68.	C	3	The number one thing all teachers should consider FIRST are the standards. Remember, no matter what, the teacher should be pushing the student towards standards mastery. Also, the state

#	Answer	Comp	Explanation
			wants to ensure that teachers, especially those who take the FTCE, are using the standards to guide instruction.
69.	C	3	Answer choice C has all the good words in an ideal answer choice: differentiated instruction, supplemental materials, and accommodate.
70.	D	3	Tier 1 interventions are what all students receive. Tier 2 interventions are what some students receive. Tier 3 interventions are what few students receive. See multi-tiered system of supports in competency 3.
71.	A	4	Before an ESE student can be suspended from school, the assistant principal must set up a manifestation determination review. This is a meeting at which a team decides if a student's misbehavior is a result of his or her disability. If the misbehavior is a result of the student's disability, the student cannot be suspended. Instead the student must receive remediation and interventions.
72.	C	4	Effective anecdotal evidence is specific details that tells the IEP team or others exactly what the student is doing. The only answer choice that is specific enough is C. The others are too general.
73.	A	4	Ice cream is considered an extrinsic reward. In addition, she is asking the group to participate in the incentive. Therefore, A is the best answer. Extrinsic rewards are things like money, play time, or candy. Intrinsic rewards are things like feeling good after completing work, feeling fulfilled after helping someone, or feeling happy after achieving goals.
74.	B	4	Tally systems are used to count how many times something happened. Therefore, B is the best answer here.
75.	C	4	One of the main tenants of positive behavior support is to reward good behavior and focus on what the student is doing well. This is supposed to encourage the student to use positive behaviors over negative ones.
76.	D	4	The teacher and the student are drawing up a contract together. That is the first clue. In addition, there are contingencies on the student's behavior, both positive and negative. This is not planned ignoring because the students behavior, good or bad, will be addressed. It is not negative practice; that is a nonsense answer choice. Finally, it is not positive consequences because the student will receive negative consequences when he displays negative behavior. D is the best answer choice here.
77.	B	4	Before the teacher can adequately address the behavior, she needs to fully understand the behavior. She must collect the data. In this case, the data is the observation of behavior. Therefore, B is the best answer here.

#	Answer	Comp	Explanation
78.	D	4	Positive behavior support (PBS) is a set of researched-based strategies used to increase the quality of life and decrease problem behaviors by teaching new skills and making changes in the person's environment to support positive behavior.
79.	A	4	A functional behavior assessment is a comprehensive and individualized strategy to identify the purpose or function of a student's problem behavior(s), develop and implement a plan to modify variables that maintain the problem behavior, and teach appropriate replacement behaviors using positive interventions. The steps for a functional behavior assessment are: define problem, collect data, analyze the data, design and implement a behavior plan (it is best to include the student in this), and monitor the plan throughout its implementation.
80.	C	4	Step number one in any situation where students are expected to behave or perform is to set clear and explicit expectations. Students cannot do what teachers want unless they know. This is not just for ESE students; this is for anyone who is working in a classroom.
81.	B	4	Designing a behavior contract ***with*** the student is key. This helps the student take ownership of the plan. Answer choice A is punitive and leaves the student out of the planning process. Sending the student to a self-contained classroom is the opposite of what should be done (remember LRE!). Never ask the principal to fix behavior problems in the classroom. That is the teacher's job.
82.	D	4	Modeling appropriate behavior and praising specific behaviors is much more effective in helping students behave appropriately than any other choice here. Calling the principal to come in is temporary and ineffective. Tally systems are great for MTSS, but the word *regulate* is negative. Reading stories on good behavior is ok, but not as effective as modeling and praise.
83.	B	4	Ignoring negative behavior and specifically praising positive behavior is effective in helping students behave appropriately.
84.	D	4	Intrinsic rewards are the most effective way to inspire students to use appropriate behavior. Intrinsic rewards include feelings of accomplishment, achievement and growth. In this case D is the only intrinsic reward out of the four.
85.	A	5	Echolalia is the meaningless repetition of words and is often associated with autism.
86.	C	5	Pragmatics is the branch of language development where students use the rules of language in different contexts. It is a high-level skill. Pre-alphabetic and partial alphabetic (A and B) are the beginning stages of language. Syntax has to do with spelling.
87.	D	5	Phonemic segmentation is breaking down words by sounds. In this case, the word CAT is broken down by each sound: C-A-T. Phonics

#	Answer	Comp	Explanation
			has to do with spelling. Semantic has to do with meaning. Pre-alphabetic has to do with skills students have before they understand the alphabet—seeing a picture of a sun and knowing it is a sun.
88.	C	5	Etymology is the study of root words and their origin. Because these words all have the same root (*cred-*). Etymology is the best choice here.
89.	A	5	CVC words are words made up of consonant, vowel, consonant. CVCC are words made up of consonant, vowel, consonant, consonant. And so on. This approach is systematic because the teacher is starting with the easiest words and moving to the more difficult words. Semantic, metacognition and comprehension have to do with meaning.
90.	C	5	The teacher is modeling the reading process in this scenario. Decoding is sounding out words. Semantic mapping is looking at meaning in text or in words. Structural analysis is breaking up words or phrases. Modeling is the best answer here.
91.	D	5	Morphology is the study of words, how they are formed, and their relationship to other words. Morphology requires students to analyze the structure of words and parts of words, such as stems, root words, prefixes, and suffixes.
92.	A	5	All the individual skills in this question fit under the umbrella of phonological awareness. Phonological awareness is a broad set of skills that includes identifying and manipulating units of oral language—parts such as phonemes in words, syllables, and onsets and rimes. Students with phonological awareness also understand conventional spelling. Remember, phonemic awareness is a sub-skill of phonological awareness and only deals with the smallest unit of sound, the phoneme. Phonics is just spelling, and structural analysis is breaking apart words.
93.	B	5	Semantics is all about meaning. Answer choice B has the word "mean" in it. The other three answer choices are not about meaning in the text.
94.	C	5	Remember, phonemic awareness is a sub-skill of phonological awareness. While the terms are often used synonymously, they are not the same thing. When a student can recognize and pronounce individual sounds in words, or phonemes, he or she is demonstrating phonemic awareness. The other choices are indicative of phonological awareness.
95.	B	4	Metacognition is ***thinking*** about ***thinking***. Cognition relates to the brain and thinking. Read aloud/think aloud is the best choice. It has the word *think* in the title of the strategy.

#	Answer	Comp	Explanation
96.	D	5	Match your Blooms verbs here. You see the phrase *critical thinking* in the question stem, find words like *evaluate, analyze, and apply* in the answer choices.
97.	B	5	Because the student is in 3rd grade, the most appropriate way for him to show comprehension is by drawing a picture. Multiple-choice test is rarely the answer on this exam. Writing an essay is developmentally inappropriate for this student. Identifying vocab is not about comprehension. B is the best answer.
98.	A	5	To increase automaticity in anything, the skill must be repeated. Repeated reading is the best answer here.
99.	A	5	Choral reading provides built-in support for those students who may feel self-conscious reading aloud. During this unison reading, students' fluency is supported as they build speed, prosody, and accuracy and is a non-threatening, low-risk way for students to practice and build confidence.
100.	B	5	Children at this stage memorize the visual features of words and can guess them in context/environmental print. However, when the words are shown to the child without the environmental cues, the child cannot read the word because he or she has not made the necessary connections between the phonemes and graphemes. In full-alphabetic (**A**), children can decode unfamiliar words and store sight words in memory. In partial-alphabetic (**C**), children recognize some letter-sound connections and can use them in context to remember words by sight. In consolidated-alphabetic (**D**), children recognize larger units of blended sound that recur in different words.
101.	D	5	Independent reading is considered >95%.
102.	A	5	Breaking down words by their structure (prefixes, suffixes, and roots) is a structural analysis.
103.	C	5	Directionality in reading is from left to right.
104.	C	5	Conferencing with students and coming up with a plan cooperatively is the best way to empower students to take charge of their own learning. Students are more likely to follow curriculum and adhere to expectations when they have the opportunity engage in the planning process of curriculum and their learning path.
105.	D	5	Rubrics should be available to students to convey expectations before they start the assignment. They should also be available to students during the writing assignment so students can reference expectations while they write. Finally, rubrics should be available after the assignment to show students how they scored according to the rubric.
106.	B	5	The question says *text-to-text*. **B** fits that criteria.

#	Answer	Comp	Explanation
107.	B	5	Literature circles are used to facilitate collaborative learning with student-centered inquiry. Students read and analyze text together. Every student has a job within the group.
108.	C	5	The teacher is using modeling, but more specifically she is using a strategy called read aloud/think aloud. Decoding is sounding out words. Semantic mapping is looking at meaning in text or in words. Structural analysis is breaking up words or phrases. Modeling is the best answer here.
109.	A	5	Studying words in context helps students to relate the context to the meaning. It is an effective way to help students connect with words.
110.	A	5	Journals allow students to share their feelings in a private setting. Journals are a positive way to relate text to life experiences. The other three answer choices are not a good fit for text-to-self connections.
111.	D	6	These skills are considered functional because they are used for success in the real-world. These skills allow students to be independent in their daily lives.
112.	C	6	This is considered supported employment because she will receive additional training and support. Job shadowing is when a person follows another throughout the work day. Sheltered employment involves holding a job but in a protected environment. Career education refers to vocational training for a specific job field and that training happens in school.
113.	B	6	Self-determination is the ability to identify and achieve goals based on a foundation of *knowing and valuing oneself*. Students must make choices, take control, believe in themselves and act in a manner that helps them achieve in school and career.
114.	C	6	Interest inventories provide information about an individual's preferences for certain careers, occupational activities, or types of work.
115.	A	6	The transition IEP is used for a student age 16 and older. The transition IEP helps prepare a student for life after school. Planning for the transition IEP should begin when the student is 14.
116.	D	6	Remember, do not pick any answer choices that sound punitive or unreasonable on this test. Answers A, B and C are punitive. Answer choice D includes the student and works with the student to overcome a bad situation.
117.	A	6	Self-advocacy is the ability to speak and act on behalf of one's self. Self-advocacy is an important skill ESE students must exercise when attending IEP meetings or deciding how to move forward with their goals.

#	Answer	Comp	Explanation
118.	A	6	Transition planning is used to coordinated sets of activities for a student with disabilities that is a results-oriented process focused on the student's post-secondary pursuits—jobs, college.
119.	D	6	The goal is to help students function independently in the real-world.
120.	B	6	In an apprenticeship, the student is exposed to job skills the student can immediately use.

This page is left blank intentionally.

Practice Test 2

1. The Florida State Board of Education Rules confidentiality safeguards require that:
   A. all student information must be reproduced and maintained in the classroom.
   B. all student records be maintained in a secure environment.
   C. all students' parents be notified before initial evaluation.
   D. all students have access to their records.
2. What can all parties request in order to forego due process during the dispute resolution process?
   A. filing a complaint
   B. writing a formal letter
   C. contacting the district office
   D. scheduling a stakeholder mediation
3. Which of the following disorders involves difficulty understanding what others are saying?
   A. expressive language
   B. dysarthria
   C. receptive language
   D. aphasia
4. Which of the following gross motor skills does a child typically develop first?
   A. sitting up in a high chair
   B. crawling on the floor
   C. rolling over from front to back
   D. standing up independently
5. A guidance counselor is scheduling a 3-year reevaluation meeting for a student. Which of the following personnel must be invited to participate in the meeting?
   A. general education teacher
   B. assistant principal
   C. school psychologist
   D. student's lawyer
6. The Individuals with Disabilities Education Act (IDEA) puts which of the following responsibilities on a student's IEP team regarding disciplinary procedures for a student with an emotional or behavioral disability?
   A. determining if a behavior is a manifestation of the student's disability
   B. conducting a due process hearing with the student's parents
   C. protecting the student from expulsion from school regardless of the violation
   D. completing a crisis intervention report to include in the student's school records

7. A special education teacher is serving as a consultant for a student who is in full-time general education classes. Which of the following best describes the role the teacher should assume?

   A. providing availability to assist the general education teachers

   B. providing daily instruction to the student

   C. administering discipline to the student when necessary

   D. designing lessons for the student to use in each class

8. Of the following teaching models, which is most appropriate for planning to meet the needs of students with severe disabilities?

   A. individual planning

   B. parent-teacher planning

   C. school-based planning

   D. team planning

9. An IEP for a new student must include which of the following according to the Individuals with Disabilities Education Act (IDEA)?

   A. measurable annual learning goals

   B. a coordinated plan for family involvement

   C. specific instructional strategies

   D. a behavior intervention plan

10. A disproportionate number of English language learners (ELL) are placed into a lower achievement level classroom. One possibility for this is the difficulty these students have with:

   A. content area textbook vocabulary.

   B. socializing with their peers.

   C. small group testing and activities.

   D. alternate instructional materials.

11. The Individuals with Disabilities Act (IDEA) mandates that individual assessments be:

   A. administered by more than one person.

   B. administered by the referral team as a group.

   C. adapted to the nature of the student's disability.

   D. adapted and standardized for appropriateness.

12. An eligibility staffing meeting has been convened for a student who may have an intellectual disability. Which of the following is most important for the ESE teacher to voice concern over?

   A. Members of the team seek the input of nonprofessionals such as the student's family.

   B. Members base their recommendations solely on the student's IQ score.

   C. Members take anecdotal information into account when making decisions.

   D. Members express disagreement when considering IEP placement.

13. A student, who receives special education services and who has a history of misconduct, enrolls in a different school but in the same district as the previous year. After the year begins, the new school receives the student's records from the previous school and administration asks to meet with the student's parents. Administration suggests placing the students in a self-contained classroom for students with varying exceptionalities. Upset with the administration's suggestion, the parents demanded a copy of all the records the school possesses for their child. Which of the following responses is legally accurate?

    A. The parents may view the records, but the school does not have to provide a copy.

    B. The parents may not view the records until after a due process hearing.

    C. The school will provide a copy of the records after the IEP team meets.

    D. The school will provide a copy of the records within 30 days.

14. Which of the following entities is responsible for determining eligibility requirements for specific ESE categories in the Florida public schools?

    A. state board of education

    B. local county government

    C. state legislative branch

    D. district school board

15. A new paraprofessional will be working with an ESE teacher in the upcoming school year. Which of the following would be most important to focus a discussion on by the ESE teacher when meeting the paraprofessional for the first time?

    A. the teacher's educational philosophy and expectations of the paraprofessional in the classroom

    B. procedures the teacher wants the paraprofessional to follow when correcting student work

    C. specifics of the classroom schedule and the free periods assigned to the teacher and the paraprofessional

    D. academic levels of the students with whom the teacher and the paraprofessional will be working with

16. The Individuals with Disabilities Education Act (IDEA) states that certain requirements concerning dispute resolution must be specified and implemented by the

    A. federal government

    B. school district

    C. county

    D. state

17. A 1st grade teacher suspects that a student may have a disability. Based on two months of daily observations with anecdotal notes, including documentation of daily lesson plan adjustments and adaptations of material, the teacher decides to make a recommendation for ESE. Which of the following processes has the teacher been using?

    A. prereferral

    B. program development

    C. reevaluation

    D. standardized assessments

NAVAED

18. Which of the following best describes the impact of the Family Educational Rights and Privacy Act (FERPA) on the education of students with disabilities?

A. Students must be provided with appropriate transportation to and from school.

B. Parents can inspect and review all educational records relating to their child.

C. Students must receive a free and appropriate education.

D. Parents can request a specific educational placement for their child.

19. An ESE student in the 2nd grade has average to above average intellectual abilities, low average to average academic achievement, and attention-deficit hyperactivity disorder (ADHD) that is successfully treated with medication. Which of the following would be the most appropriate placement for this student?

A. general education classroom

B. part-time classroom

C. special day school

D. full-time ese classroom

20. A teacher with paraprofessional help posts an objective on the board that describes the application of the day's lesson in the school community. The teacher proceeds to take some of the students outside for an application activity while the paraprofessional proceeds to have the other students reread the lesson aloud instead of performing the activity. Which of the following best reflects the learning results in this classroom?

A. Both groups are accomplishing the objective of applying the lesson content and the paraprofessional was appropriately prepared to lead the group.

B. Neither group is accomplishing the objective, the teacher will plan a follow-up lesson for both groups that will include the school community.

C. The paraprofessional's group of students is accomplishing the objective by following the plan in the lesson for both groups, but the teacher' group of students has added an extra activity.

D. The teacher's group of students is accomplishing the objective, but the paraprofessional's group of students is not. The objective of the lesson needs to be communicated more clearly to the paraprofessional.

21. Which of the following groups of people reflect an IEP team?

A. teachers, the ESE student, the parents of the ESE student, a local pediatrician

B. teachers, the ESE student, the parents of the ESE student, the student's speech pathologist

C. teachers, the ESE student, the parents of the ESE student, community members

D. teachers, the ESE student, the parents of the ESE student, the ESE student's peers

22. Which of the following is a component of consultative services for ESE students?

A. co-teaching model in a specialized classroom

B. direct communication with the student's general education teacher

C. assistive technology in a self-contained classroom

D. consultation with the parents on a weekly basis

23. A student is repeating phrases and noises in the classroom. What symptom is this student displaying?

    A. ADHD
    B. apraxia
    C. dysarthria
    D. echolalia

24. A 3rd grade English language learner (ELL) with an intellectual disability has been identified for placement in the ESE program. When writing the initial IEP for this student, which of the following is the most appropriate language consideration?

    A. requiring all instructions to be in English
    B. providing access to a dual language dictionary for testing
    C. requiring the use of a communication board
    D. providing heritage language support to the student

25. Which of the following is the most appropriate step for an ESE teacher to take in ensuring paraprofessionals are properly prepared?

    A. providing a written statement of duties
    B. getting paired with other teacher aides
    C. conducting informal conversations
    D. creating video feedback

26. Scheduling concerns and fragmentation of speech and language services are two problems associated with:

    A. classroom-based speech and language model.
    B. strategies-based approach.
    C. team-teaching approach.
    D. pullout therapy model.

27. Which of the following is one of the main avenues individuals with disabilities have achieved constitutional rights?

    A. recommendation by the federal government
    B. telephone campaign
    C. formation of advocacy groups
    D. public awareness

28. A general education teacher has set up a meeting with an ESE teacher to go over some concerns about being able to meet the needs of two of her ESE students. Early in the meeting the ESE teacher detects resistance coming from the general education teacher about what she is telling her. Which of the following would be the ESE teacher's best initial response?

    A. volunteering in the general education classroom to work with the students
    B. interrupting the meeting and requesting the presence of a school administrator
    C. offering to increase the amount of time the students spend in the resource room
    D. expressing willingness to confer about the student regularly with the teacher

29. An ESE student identified with emotional or behavioral disability is under the supervision of a caregiver. In an effort to help the child overcome the impact of the disability, the caregiver receives parent and caregiver training and counseling. The caregiver is receiving which of the following services?

    A. related services

    B. early intervention services

    C. supplementary aids and services

    D. nonviolent crisis intervention services

30. Test validity is best described as the extent to which an assessment:

    A. reduces cultural and ethnic bias.

    B. discriminates the results among test takers.

    C. measures what it is supposed to measure.

    D. produces consistent results across different administrations.

31. A 5th grade ESE student has a pattern of turning in homework assignments on Tuesday through Thursday but forgetting on Monday and Friday. To help the student the ESE teacher sets a target behavior of compliance to turning in homework five days a week. In collaboration with the behavior specialist, the teacher breaks down the steps required to complete the task (e.g. writing down the assignment, bringing home material) and provides reinforcement as the student performs the steps. This situation is an example of which of the following positive behavior management concepts?

    A. fading

    B. shaping

    C. probing

    D. modeling

32. Anecdotal observation can help teachers identify the function of a student's target behavior by

    A. finding patterns in the antecedents and consequences of the behavior

    B. determining whether the student can self-identify the problem behavior

    C. measuring how disruptive the student's behavior is to the class

    D. providing historical data regarding the problem

33. An ESE teacher collected observational data on a student with attention deficits and realized the student had not completed even one task in two weeks. To begin a proactive intervention, the teacher shortened the student's assignments and provided support and verbal praise as each task was completed. The student is now able to complete assignments independently. The teacher's next step in the intervention should be to

    A. Have the student begin recording each completed task on a chart.

    B. Adjust the schedule of praise for every assignment to praise for every other assignment.

    C. Resume giving the student full-length assignments.

    D. Establish a system of visual prompts to remind the student to complete each task.

34. Formal observation data collected by a 5th grade teacher indicates that a student with high functioning autism spectrum disorder shouts out answers an average of ten times per hour. The classroom teacher consults with the ESE teacher regarding strategies to address this problem. Which of the following strategies should the ESE teacher suggest first?

A. verbally reminding the student to raise their hand each time the student fails to do so

B. providing the student with a visual prompt to raise hand and reinforce the proper behavior

C. have the student write a paragraph explaining why it is important not to shout out during discussions

D. arranging for the student to go to a time out area whenever the student shouts out an answer

35. A student with emotional behavioral disability has been placed in a collaborative, heterogenous group for small-group instruction. Throughout the class the student places tick marks across the top of his paper. Suddenly, the student approaches the teacher and asks to be moved to an individual desk. What is this an example of?

A. self-monitoring

B. refusal of class rules

C. voluntary reassignment

D. random disruptive behavior

36. Which of the following assessment situations provides an example of test bias for a student who recently arrived from another country and speaks limited English?

A. an achievement test that is administered in the student's heritage language

B. a teacher designed unit test that is administered primarily by a language interpreter

C. a state achievement test that is administered with only the accommodation of extended time

D. a standardized intelligence test that is administered and is normed on a group with characteristics matching the student's background

37. Testing accommodations for students with disabilities are based on:

A. the requests of the student or student's parents.

B. what a student needs to access the assessments.

C. the effect of the individual student's exceptionality.

D. what classroom environment the student is placed in.

38. An ESE teacher chooses to administer an informal reading inventory to determine a student's reading level. This informal reading inventory is an appropriate assessment tool for this purpose because it will:

A. provide information about the student's reading strategies.

B. compare the student's performance to his/her classmates.

C. give the student an opportunity to benefit from the teacher prompts.

D. indicate the student's grade level compared to a normed sample.

39. An ESE teacher has noticed her student has become disengaged and disruptive during class. What would be the best evidence the teacher can bring to the IEP meeting to address this issue?

A. anecdotal classroom behavior data

B. survey data from other students

C. discipline referral data

D. attendance records

40. Ms. Jones, a general education teacher, has several ESE students in her class. What is she required to do prior to starting instruction for these students?

A. Consult with the school counselor about strategies she can use to serve her students.

B. Read each ESE student's IEP and indicate, in her lesson plans, how she will accommodate those students.

C. Reach out to the parents and ask how she can accommodate the students.

D. Ask for a paraprofessional to come into the class and serve the students who need it.

41. Which of the following accommodations is NOT permitted to be used on a state-assessment?

A. On a reading assessment, a student is given extra time to complete the passage.

B. On a reading assessment, a teacher reads the passage aloud to the student.

C. On a reading assessment, a teacher reads the questions aloud to the student.

D. On a reading assessment, the student is permitted to take the exam in a private room.

42. Which of the following would be an example of assessment bias?

A. Designing different forms of a test to meet the needs of students in a multicultural environment

B. Creating a mathematics test with 20 word problems about boys building items such as forts and doghouses

C. Preparing an electronic recording that gives students background information needed to understand items on a test

D. Developing a test on a computer using a screen reader for students with limited reading skills

43. An ESE teacher wants to track student progress on a weekly basis. Which of the following is the best type of assessment to use?

A. project-based informal assessment

B. norm-referenced formal assessment

C. curriculum-based informal assessment

D. criterion-referenced formal assessment

44. A 9th grade ESE student scored a 53-percentile rank on a standardized test. When discussing the result with the student, the teacher should explain that:

A. the student answered 53% of the test questions correctly.

B. the student scored better than 53% of students testing on the same day.

C. the student scored better than 53% of students in the norming group.

D. the student answered 53% of the questions on the test.

45. A 5th grade student with specific learning disabilities has shown minimal academic improvement since the beginning of the year. The ESE teacher is now identifying specific deficit areas using techniques such as modeling, holding conferences with the student, providing prompts and cues, and asking what the student is thinking. Which of the following approaches is the teacher using?

A. task analysis

B. behavior contracting

C. dynamic assessment

D. cooperative learning

46. In a school system where the population of students is culturally diverse, which of the following would be LEAST likely incorporated into a lesson to reduce any cultural bias within the classroom?

A. dividing the class into groups based on language abilities

B. allowing students to share their own experiences

C. providing information about different cultures represented in the school

D. sharing personal feelings about beliefs

47. A 6th grade student with a significant disability has difficulty using a spoon for eating and mimicking or copying behavior that is modeled by others. Which of the following types of prompting would be most beneficial for the student at this time?

A. spoken prompt

B. pictorial prompt

C. gestural prompt

D. physical prompt

48. An ESE teacher's primary consideration when selecting an appropriate instructional practice should be:

A. determining the amount of time the practice will require.

B. ensuring that colleagues in the school accept the practice.

C. determining whether the students are familiar with the practice.

D. ensuring that research has shown the practice to be effective.

49. A newly hired ESE teacher has been placed in a challenging class where behavior management techniques are not always successful. The teacher would like to self-assess his own strengths and weaknesses in order to become a more effective teacher. Which of the following should the teacher do first to address this goal more effectively?

A. Attend a professional development workshop on behavior management.

B. Read current articles in special education journals about behavior management techniques.

C. Incorporate the behavior management strategies of more experienced special education teachers.

D. Record different behavior management methods that have been used in class and reflect in a journal.

50. Which of the following is a part of the procedural dimension of classroom management?

A. conveying enthusiasm to students about learning

B. arranging furniture to allow efficient traffic flow

C. allowing student input in monitoring target behaviors

D. establishing a consistent routine for submitting work

51. A 3rd grade student has mild intellectual and emotional or behavioral disabilities. The student has been resistant to coteaching in the inclusive classroom as well as individualized instruction. The student is well liked and has many friends in the class and also the school. The student's teacher would find the best results by initiating

A. a task analysis

B. cooperative learning strategies

C. a reduced curriculum

D. developmental teaching

52. Which of the following approaches would be most effective to meet the learning needs of all students when introducing an entirely new concept to a class of students with various disabilities?

A. direct instruction

B. indirect instruction

C. multimodal instruction

D. Cooperative instruction

53. An ESE teacher in a special needs class has the following list of actions written on the board:

Partially tighten shoelaces, vertically pull shoelaces tight, cross shoelaces, tie into a knot, make a bow, and tighten bow.

This is an example of:

A. functional behavior assessment.

B. task analysis.

C. measurable goals.

D. social skills instruction.

54. The English, math, science, and social studies ESE inclusion teachers of a high school share approximately 75% of the same students. The social studies teacher is beginning a unit on the Great Depression and informs the other teachers. Together they create a thematic unit. The science teacher will incorporate discoveries made during the time period in class, the English teacher will incorporate literature written during the time period, and the math teacher will use problems that use equations to calculate stocks and economic trends. Which of the following instructional strategies is this an example of?

A. multimodal instruction

B. cooperative instruction

C. generalization instruction

D. cross-curricular instruction

55. Which of the following would be the best approach when trying to find an evidence-based classroom behavior management system for a teacher to implement?

A. Start with techniques simply based on experience and adding more elements as time goes by

B. Conducting research using professional materials regarding organizations or agencies in behavior management

C. Ask experienced teachers currently in the school about what works for them

D. Consulting online blogs and personal webpages of experienced leaders

56. An ESE math teacher is teaching a lesson on order of operations. She puts PEMDAS on the board and describes to the students that each letter represents the order each operation should be done when solving a problem. Which of the following strategies is the teacher demonstrating?

    A. guided notes

    B. mastery learning

    C. mnemonic device

    D. graphic organizer

57. An instructional rubric is most effective when:

    A. the teacher creates the rubric with the students and shows them how to use it.

    B. students in the class develop the rubric in cooperative learning groups.

    C. the teacher creates and applies an individual rubric for each student in the class.

    D. students in the class develop and use the rubric in homogenous pairs.

58. An ESE teacher learns about a new program at a conference she attended that claims to eliminate behavior issues during remedial reading instruction. Which of the following would be best for the teacher to collect before approaching administration about funding the program for her classroom?

    A. statistics produced by the company about the program's achievements

    B. data compiled independently and published relating to the program

    C. student enthusiasm after trialing the program

    D. availability of grants to pay for the program

59. Which of the following would be appropriate to use in a portfolio assessment?

    A. discipline referrals

    B. daily journals

    C. peer reports

    D. copy of IEP

60. During an observation of the adaptive behavior of a kindergarten student, the ESE teacher notices the student does not take turns or share. Based on these observations the teacher should recommend which of the following instructional procedures first?

    A. social skill instruction

    B. community-based instruction

    C. peer-mediated instruction

    D. communication skill instruction

61. An ESE student's acquisition of general academic skills that involves the sequencing, practicing, and repeating of each skill level is supported through which teaching method?

    A. direct instruction

    B. echo reading

    C. choral reading

    D. discovery learning

62. A teacher is using intervention strategies to assist a student who has a processing disorder. She is using Tier 3 interventions which include individualized instruction for concepts in math. What is this an example of?

A. paraprofessional

B. multi-tiered system of supports

C. pull-out method

D. push-in method

63. An ESE student, who is 18 and confined to a wheelchair, has a goal outlined in her IEP for independent living skills. She wants to be able to turn on a standard light switch. Often, standard light switches are hard for her to reach from her wheelchair. What strategies can her teacher employ to help her achieve her goal?

A. Have a paraprofessional turn the lights on and off for the student because she won't be able to reach the switch from her wheelchair.

B. Provide her with an extended hand tool and allow her to practice turning on and off the light with the tool.

C. Suggest that she purchase voice-activated lighting in her home, so she can use her voice rather than her hands.

D. Request the IEP team review her goals because this goal is unreasonable considering her disability.

64. A 4th grade ESE student is working in math class. The teacher notices he is consistently writing 3s whenever he should be writing 8s. What should the teacher do?

A. Ask the paraprofessional to work with the student.

B. Bring it up at the next IEP meeting.

C. Use targeted intervention strategies in math decoding skills.

D. Pair the student with a high achieving student to fix the problem.

65. Which of the following would be the most appropriate strategy to use for students who have varying disabilities and interests?

A. flexible grouping

B. static grouping

C. heterogenous grouping

D. homogenous grouping

66. Which of the following is LEAST likely to be a factor when considering the use of instructional materials?

A. cost and accessibility

B. comprehensive teacher's edition

C. state standards and objectives

D. student interest and prior knowledge

67. In an ESE inclusion class during a lesson in language arts, half of the students are finishing early, while others are struggling to finish on time. What would be the best approach for the teacher to use in this situation.

A. Use whole group instruction where everyone gets the same instruction regardless of level.

B. Use small group instruction for those who struggle, and free time for those who finished early.

C. Use computer instruction so those who finish early can use challenging computer programs in language arts.

D. Use differentiated instruction that allows the high achievers to be challenged and allows for the struggling students to receive interventions.

68. Which of the following would be the most appropriate method to assist ESE students struggling in a general education classroom?

A. Use accommodations during instruction.

B. Make the lesson easier.

C. Use a paraprofessional.

D. Change the standards for the lesson.

69. An ESE student with emotional or behavioral disability has a low threshold of frustration. Which of the following is the most reasonable accommodation to implement on mathematics homework assignments for this student?

A. extended time for completion

B. reduced number of problems

C. taped instruction

D. modified reading level

70. A 7th grade general education classroom offers many different opportunities to show growth in interpersonal interactions. One system that the teacher uses includes charts and visuals with stated criteria and gradations at different levels of quality. This is an example of which procedure?

A. instructional rubric

B. teacher checklist

C. task analysis checklist

D. situational assessment

71. Two major components of self-management checklists are to teach students how to properly use them and to complete the checklist:

A. with fidelity.

B. in a timely manner.

C. during instructional time.

D. without the help of peers.

72. An ESE student with emotional or behavioral disability has been charged with a felony resulting from an act committed during school. Which option is legally available to the school board if the student's behavior has been determined to be related to his disability?

   A. suspension for the remainder of the school year

   B. continued services in a different setting

   C. commitment to a detention center

   D. immediate expulsion from the school

73. A child study team learns of a student who is off task a great deal of the school day from a general education teacher. The team recommends the teacher gather data on the duration and number of incidents the student is off task. Which of the following would be the most effective procedure for gathering such data?

   A. samples of portfolio

   B. direct observation techniques

   C. behavior rating scales

   D. curriculum-based assessment

74. Which of the following is an example of an anecdotal record?

   A. After the teacher finished giving instructions, it took the student 20 minutes to begin working. The student used the same mathematical operation on all 15 problems.

   B. The student was hyperactive during mathematics class and didn't comply with the teacher's instructions. The work was full of mistakes.

   C. By the time the student arrived for class, the student medication had worn off and the resulting behavior was inappropriate.

   D. The student doesn't seem to be happy in mathematics class, and the work has been terrible. The student never finishes the assignment and the work is sloppy.

75. An ESE teacher is conducting an observation for a functional behavior assessment. Which of the following is an example of an observable and measurable statement made by the teacher?

   A. The student covered her eyes.

   B. The student had a tantrum for 5 minutes.

   C. The student got excited.

   D. The student shut down.

76. Which of the following statements best expresses the rationale for a functional behavioral assessment?

   A. observing other students' response to a behavior

   B. increasing supervision to prevent a behavior

   C. determining the purpose of the behavior

   D. finding the psychological cause of a behavior

77. A high school student had to be restrained following an incident in the cafeteria in which he posed a danger to others in the immediate area. The teacher deescalated the situation to the point where administration processed the student. He later returned to class and resumed the rest of the school day. Which of the following is legally required of the teacher?

A. Notify the parents in writing the same day.

B. Move the student to seclusion to avoid further incidents.

C. Review the behavior intervention plan with the student.

D. Contact administration to update the status of the student.

78. The strategy of planned ignoring may be used by a teacher when a student continually raises his hand to receive attention or disrupt the class. Planned ignoring is more commonly referred to as

A. punishment

B. refocusing

C. extinction

D. time-out

79. A teacher using functional behavior assessment is most likely interested in:

A. determining whether behaviors observed at school are also observed at home.

B. differentiating between behavioral reinforcements that are positive and negative.

C. identifying behavior change after an intervention plan has been implemented.

D. obtaining information about the purpose a behavior serves for a student.

80. An IEP team plans to conduct a functional behavioral assessment to learn more about how a student's behavior is interfering with learning. The team is most likely to obtain information about contributing environmental factors by

A. observing the student

B. interviewing the student

C. reviewing the student's school records

D. consulting the student's previous teacher

81. After a functional behavioral analysis of a student, it is determined that the target behavior of out-of-seat behavior is used to avoid embarrassment about poor reading skills. A team member proposes a replacement behavior of allowing the student to stand instead of sitting at the desk. Which of the following is true about the replacement behavior?

A. This is an appropriate replacement behavior because it is compatible with the target behavior.

B. This is an inappropriate replacement behavior because it does not address the issue that needs to be solved.

C. This is an inappropriate replacement behavior because it does not fit with the target behavior and classroom rules and expectations.

D. This is an appropriate replacement behavior because it is similar to the target behavior and allows the student to move around.

82. Which of the following is one of the most common functions of behavior displayed by adolescents?

   A. task avoidance

   B. teacher attention

   C. sensory stimulation

   D. access to material

83. A 4th grade student exhibits both social and academic problems in an ESE classroom. Which of the following would be a key element of a behavioral intervention plan for the student?

   A. pre-correcting

   B. punishing

   C. screening

   D. reprimanding

84. In an ESE classroom, students earn points for following the class procedures. At the end of the week the students can exchange points for items in a treasure box. This is an example of

   A. response cost

   B. a behavior contract

   C. task analysis

   D. a token economy

85. Which of the following types of assistive technology would best enable a student with quadriplegia and a speech impairment to participate actively in learning activities?

   A. touch-screen computer monitor

   B. text-to-speech software

   C. desktop publishing program

   D. electronic communication device

86. An ESE student has difficulty pulling together a variety of vocabulary words into proper usage to create a sentence structure that describes something or presents and idea. This is an example of

   A. word-finding deficit

   B. word definition deficit

   C. expressive language deficit

   D. receptive language deficit

87. A 14-year-old ESE student with a profound intellectual disability and moderate hearing loss communicates by using one- and two-word phrases. The student struggles with articulation due to the hearing loss. Which of the following communication systems would best allow the student to have functional communication skills?

   A. alternative keyboard

   B. word prediction software

   C. word abbreviations

   D. communication board

88. A 2nd grade ESE student is not demonstrating typical language development. The student has difficulty staying on topic when having a conversation and taking turns with peers. In which component of language structure is the student demonstrating a deficit?

A. semantics

B. phonology

C. pragmatics

D. morphology

89. An ESE student is nonverbal and has autism spectrum disorder. The IEP team has determined that the student needs a low-tech assistive technology in order to improve interactions with others. Which of the following would be best for the student to assist with interacting with others?

A. picture exchange communication system

B. multi-button voice output device

C. step-by-step sequencer

D. interactive software

90. An ESE teacher is working with a 5th grade student in a resource room. The student's class is about to start reading a history charter on a topic unfamiliar to the student. To promote the student's reading comprehension, what would be the teacher's most effective first step?

A. Remind the student to study carefully.

B. Develop the student's background knowledge.

C. Teach the student outlining skills.

D. Review the student's metacognitive strategies.

91. An ESE student with attention deficit hyperactivity disorder (ADHD) has an above-grade level academic vocabulary but reads slowly and has difficulty with reading comprehension. What specific effect does ADHD have on reading comprehension?

A. Processing speed

B. Oculomotor rapidity

C. Automaticity issues

D. Prefrontal misconnection

92. When assisting students in selecting books to use for silent sustained reading time, a teacher should help them choose books that fall into which of the following levels?

A. Independent

B. Instructional

C. Supported

D. Frustration

93. Which of the following is the most appropriate consideration for selecting materials and activities for a school district with a very culturally diverse population to align with all standards and promote success?

A. socio-economic

B. language spoken

C. student interest

D. gender ratio

94. An ESE student in a 9th grade social studies class has difficulty listening to presentations and taking notes simultaneously. Which of the following adaptations could the teacher make to best help the student?

   A. Allow the student to make audio recordings of the lectures.

   B. Seat the student in the front row of the classroom.

   C. Test the student only on material addressed in the textbook.

   D. Deliver speeches at a significantly reduced price.

95. An English language learner (ELL) has scored low on a standardized reading assessment. Before referring the student for placement in a program for specific learning disabilities, the response to intervention (RTI) team must first determine whether the

   A. child will benefit from the added support.

   B. child has sufficient language skills to benefit from the program.

   C. assessment results will impact scores on a national rating.

   D. assessment measured learning difficulties or cultural differences.

96. Several English language learners (ELLs) with intellectual disabilities have been placed in an inclusion classroom where two teachers work together. What is this instructional model called?

   A. Pullout services

   B. Coordinative services

   C. Collaborative services

   D. Integrated services

97. A 4th grade ESE student struggles with reading at grade level. To build fluency, the student needs to practice reading lower level text. Which of the following techniques would best help the student be less reluctant to read the lower text at school?

   A. recording text with the teacher

   B. echo-reading text with the teacher

   C. rereading text multiple times with a classmate

   D. buddy-reading text with a 2nd grade student

98. An ESE student in an inclusion reading class is struggling with more complex reading passages. The teacher implements a differentiation strategy to assist the student. The teacher begins to demonstrate how to chunk a complex reading passage into smaller portions. Next, the student has to read the passage using the demonstrated chunking method. While the student reads the passage the teacher offers positive, corrective feedback. After the teacher identifies that the student understands the chunking method, the teacher begins to fade the prompts and feedback to increase the student's independence. Which of the following types of differentiation methods is this an example of?

   A. modeling

   B. scaffolding

   C. guided practice

   D. constructivist method

99. A 19-year old ESE student with an intellectual disability reads at a 4th grade level and has difficulty spelling most words. Which of the following areas should a majority of the student's spelling words for class be taken?

A. words containing common blends

B. early elementary word lists

C. words with regular spelling

D. functional word lists

100. An ESE teacher uses the following approach to teach spelling skills to a small group of students in the resource room: hear the word, see the word, write the word, check the word.

What approach is being used?

A. metacognition

B. overlearning

C. multi-sensory

D. naturalistic

101. Which of the following learning strategies is most appropriate for a student with a disability whose written work is characterized by incomplete sentences and improper use of punctuation and capitalization?

A. word identification

B. error monitoring

C. paraphrasing

D. multipass

102. A new student comes to the classroom with assistive technology. The teacher doesn't know how to use it and places it on a shelf in the back of the classroom. What is likely to happen?

A. The student's progress will start to decline over the course of the next few weeks.

B. The student will adapt without the assistive technology and overcome the disability.

C. The student's progress will remain the same with or without the assistive technology.

D. The teacher will be fired immediately for not adhering to the student's IEP.

103. A teacher can best develop children's self-confidence and positive feelings toward learning by providing activities that:

A. present a limited level of difficulty.

B. exceed developmental capabilities.

C. reward students when they answer questions correctly.

D. provide challenges while also offering opportunities for success.

104. Many ESE students in a 3rd grade class have poor listening skills. The teacher wants to assist students in developing better listening skills, so they can be successful in the classroom. Which of the following pairs of strategies would be most appropriate?

A. rewards for good listening skills; role play

B. concise and explicit directions; visual representations

C. visual representations; cooperative learning

D. positive reinforcement; negative consequences

105. A teacher is using augmentative and alternative communication strategies in her classroom to assist several of her ESE students. She is using outcomes of a recent assessment to make decisions in her classroom. What would be the most important question to consider when analyzing the outcome data?

A. What effects did the strategies have on the students in various academic areas?

B. How did the students feel about the strategies used during this time?

C. Are the communication device systems natural sounding and not computerized?

D. Did the students increase their ability in communication standards?

106. The most effective way to introduce vocabulary to students is to have them:

A. relate vocabulary words to relevant experiences.

B. listen to guest speakers from other countries.

C. copy down vocabulary from the glossary.

D. memorize vocabulary words.

107. A teacher is evaluating essays based on grammar and mechanics. What type of analysis is this?

A. syntactic

B. semantic

C. phonemic

D. phonological

108. An ESE teacher is helping students understand rhyme in words. She uses words like *sound*, *found*, *hound*, and *round*. She and the students are working on a lesson that focuses on:

A. phonemic awareness.

B. phonics.

C. semantic analysis.

D. syntactic analysis.

109. A third grade ESE student with a severe learning disability has just learned how to use letters correctly to write his name. What stage of writing is the student in?

A. pre-alphabetic

B. automatic

C. emergent

D. fluent

110. When students memorize high-frequency words, they are engaging in:

A. decoding

B. sight word recognition

C. onset rhyme

D. structural analysis

111. An ESE teacher with a class of students with severe disabilities develops a lesson plan that requires students to go to the local store to shop for groceries. Which of the following describes this type of instruction?

A. project-based instruction

B. life skills-based instruction

C. curriculum-based instruction

D. community-based instruction

112. The teacher of a class of ESE students with intellectual disabilities schedules a trip to the local grocery store. The reason for the trip is to link the previous classroom instruction to real world use of the skills learned. Which of the following is this an example of?

A. accommodation

B. generalization

C. presentation

D. modification

113. Rights provided under IDEA to parents of a student with a disability transfer to the student at the age of majority. In Florida, this occurs at what age?

A. 14

B. 16

C. 18

D. 21

114. An IEP is considered a transitional IEP when the student's IEP date falls within:

A. During the child's 16th birthday year

B. During the child's graduation year

C. The child's freshman year in high school

D. During the child's 18th birthday year

115. A teacher is planning a lesson for her ESE students on making a shopping list before going to the grocery store. What category does this fall under?

A. Cognitive skills

B. Metacognitive skills

C. Behavior skills

D. Life skills

116. Which of the following is most appropriate for a life-skills class where students are focusing on tasks necessary to be successful in a job?

A. Watch a video on proper employment etiquette.

B. Engage in roleplay activities that mirror employment duties.

C. Read the classifieds and research jobs available.

D. Listen to a guest speaker about interviewing for a job.

117. An ESE student has been diagnosed with Tourette's Syndrome. He often yells profanity in the class. The teacher speaks with the other students in the class about the behavior and instructs them to disregard the yelling and profanity. This is an example of:

A. planned ignoring

B. contingency contracting

C. positive behavior support

D. positive consequences

118. Which of the following is the most effective way teachers can help students develop positive self-concepts?

A. Set short-term and long-term goals and celebrating student gains.

B. Use data walls to track student progress.

C. Help students pass standardized tests.

D. Reward students when they achieve goals.

119. Which of the following would be most effective in helping students build self-determination skills?

A. Have students work on their self-esteem by reading about ESE.

B. Have students identify successful people who also have disabilities.

C. Have students pair up with other ESE students during difficult tasks.

D. Make lessons easier so ESE students feel good about themselves.

120. Self-advocacy skills involve:

A. students helping other students.

B. teachers helping students

C. students standing up for themselves.

D. students standing up for other students.

#	Answer	Comp	Explanation
1.	B	1	The Florida State Board of Education rules state that a school principal is responsible for the privacy and security of all student records maintained in the school. C pertains to Procedural Safeguards and D pertains to FERPA. There is no rule that justifies A.
2.	D	1	According to the procedural safeguards, the school district must make mediation available whether or not a due process complaint is filed. The State is responsible for all costs associated with mediation meetings.
3.	C	1	Receptive language disorder is when a student has difficulty understanding oral language or in listening. A is when a student has difficulty conveying or expressing information in speech or writing. B is when a student is difficult to understand due to slow or slurred speech. D is when a student has a language impairment affecting production or comprehension of speech and the ability to read and write.
4.	C	1	Typical developmental order would be C, A, B, D.
5.	A	1	The key term in this question is "must." All of these people may attend an IEP, but regardless if it is a regular or re-evaluation, the general education teacher MUST always attend.
6.	A	1	In dealing with disciplinary procedures, it is always the IEP team's responsibility to determine if behavior is a manifestation of the disability. B, C, and D are part of the responsibility of the IEP team, but not mandated by IDEA.
7.	A	1	The role of a special education teacher on consult is to provide the general education teacher with services and supports as needed. B, C, and D are only the responsibility of the general education teacher in the classroom.
8.	D	1	Team planning occurs when all stakeholders work together and come to a consensus on a severely disabled student's IEP supports, accommodations, and adaptations. It is the most appropriate in this situation.
9.	A	1	An IEP is most notably known for the goals and accommodations. B and C are not required in any IEP and D is only required for behavioral students and not found in every IEP.
10.	A	1	Content area vocabulary is very difficult for ELL's to comprehend without proper accommodations. As they perform poorly in these classes, they are tracked into remediation courses and thus lumped into these programs disproportionately. C and D provide aid for ELL's to succeed and B would have a negative effect on achievement.

#	Answer	Comp	Explanation
11.	C	1	IDEA allows for individual assessments to be adapted to accommodate a student's disability. A and B are incorrect because it doesn't matter how many people administer an assessment or if it's by the referral team. D is incorrect because of the standardization and it cannot be adapted.
12.	B	1	There are multiple factors that must be taken into consideration when determining eligibility for services. IQ score alone cannot be a reason for eligibility. A, C, and D are all factors that are relevant to the placement of a student for services.
13.	A	1	According to FERPA, schools are not required to provide copies of records unless, for reasons such as great distance, it is impossible for parents to review the records. Since the question states the parents met with the administrator, they had the opportunity to view the records. B, C, and D do not comply with FERPA.
14.	A	1	Eligibility requirements for ESE categories are determined by the State Board of Education. Each school district is responsible for providing services to students which is why D is incorrect. B and C deal with funding issues related to ESE programs.
15.	D	1	Although all of the answers have some merit to them D is the best and pertains to the students and the para's assignment. A is incorrect because the teacher's educational philosophy is not relevant. B is incorrect because paraprofessionals are not supposed to grade student work. Although scheduling is important, C is incorrect because D is the better answer. Remember, it is always about the student.
16.	B	1	The School District is the first entity to deal with dispute resolution according to Procedural Safeguards. A and D do not get involved unless necessary and C has no involvement.
17.	A	1	Before a student can be referred for services, a prereferral process must take place where data is compiled over a period of time containing observations and anecdotal notes. B and C happen after the disability has been determined. D is not relevant to the question.
18.	B	1	Under FERPA, parents and/or eligible guardians have the right to inspect and review the student's education records maintained by the school. Answers C and D refer to IDEA and A is the responsibility of the school district.
19.	A	1	According to Least Restrictive Environment (LRE), removal from a general education classroom is only warranted when the severity of the handicap cannot be accommodated by supplementary aids and services. The student is receiving medication for ADHD and is performing average. B, C, and D does not meet least restrictive environment.

#	Answer	Comp	Explanation
20.	D	1	The purpose of the paraprofessional is to support the general education teacher by following directions explicitly. When in doubt the teacher should conference with the paraprofessional. A and C are incorrect because the paraprofessional did not complete the objective and B is incorrect because the teacher accomplished the objective.
21.	B	1	Community members and students' friends or peers are not typically on an IEP team. In addition, a local pediatrician is not part of the team, unless the pediatrician is the student's doctor and directly related to the student's exceptionality. The best answer here is B because the student's speech pathologist would be directly related to the student's exceptionality.
22.	B	1	A student who is receiving consultative services is in a general classroom but receives services when needed or on a consult basis. Therefore, the team should be in direct communication with the student's general education teachers. When thinking consultative, think general education.
23.	D	1	Echolalia is the repetition of vocalizations. This is often done by students who are on the autism spectrum. Tourette's Syndrome is when a student involuntarily yells or screams words or profanity. Apraxia is an oral motor speech disorder affecting an individual's ability to translate conscious speech. Dysarthria is when the muscles of the mouth or face have difficulty moving.
24.	D	1	Pay close attention to the wording of the problem when it says "most appropriate" and "initial IEP." B, C, and D are all reasonable answers except D is the <u>most</u> appropriate. A is not something that needs to be done for an ELL student.
25.	C	1	Due to the nature of disabilities and the dynamic learning styles of ESE students, paraprofessionals are best prepared when they are informed through informal conversations. A is too static and does not allow for adaptation on behalf of the paraprofessional. B does not provide information from the actual ESE teacher and D works after the fact and is a tool for critiquing rather than preparation.
26.	D	1	A, B, and C all have to do with methods performed in the classroom or stationary setting. The pullout model takes planning and resources that is sometimes out of the control of teachers. For example, times may change and the teacher or paraprofessional may not be consistent in delivering services.
27.	C	1	Advocacy groups were the basis for creating awareness of the issues associated with students with disabilities. Although A, B, and D did help, they were not as instrumental.
28.	D	1	The key word in this question is "initial response." Supporting the general education teacher is the first step to help ease resistance with the ESE students. A is not correct because volunteering

#	Answer	Comp	Explanation
			should not be the first option, although it could be done later on in the process. B is also incorrect because the meeting has not escalated to that point that an administrator needs to be present. C is incorrect because a change in the IEP would be required and it impedes with least restrictive environment.
29.	A	1	We often associate related services to the different types of therapy given i.e. speech and physical to the disabled student. Related services do include parent counseling and training. B and D do not pertain to this type of situation. C deals with aids such as hearing aids, speech to text computers and any other aid or service to accommodate a student's disability.
30.	C	2	Test validity is when a test measures what it claims to measure. A and B refer to testing bias and D refers to test reliability.
31.	B	2	Shaping is a technique that involves the teacher rewarding or providing reinforcement to the student as he successfully improves the acquisition of a target skill. The key words in the problem are "provides reinforcement." A is when the teacher gradually lessens something, usually reinforcement. C is when the teacher guides students as they perform a task. D deals more with modeling a behavior, not a task.
32.	A	2	Anecdotal observations are narratives about behaviors, skills, and incidents in the classroom. They are used to determine what stimulates behavior (antecedents) and the consequences. B, C, and D are valid choices, but A is more detailed and the best choice.
33.	B	2	The teacher has implemented shaping with the student with success and now it is time to use fading where reinforcement is gradually lessened. A, C, and D are not part of the fading strategy.
34.	B	2	Prompting and providing reinforcement are the best ways to decrease target behavior. A takes too much time for the teacher and is distracting to other students. C is not a proper way to correct the behavior. D is never an option because negative consequences are never the answer.
35.	A	2	A strategy used often with EBD students is self-monitoring. Because the student puts marks on the top of his paper and asks to be moved, self-monitoring behavior is demonstrated. B is not relevant to the situation, C would have been the answer if the student moved without permission from the teacher to get away from distracting behavior, and D does not pertain to this situation.
36.	C	2	In this scenario, having only the extended time accommodation and not a language accommodation shows assessment bias and makes it unfair for the student. All of the other answers allow for fairness through language and matching the student's background.
37.	C	2	It is important to remember that all accommodations are designed for each individual based on the effect of the exceptionality. Parents

#	Answer	Comp	Explanation
			can make requests, but they may not be suitable for testing situations. B and C are the results of accommodations.
38.	D	2	An informal reading inventory (IRI) is a diagnostic assessment tool meant to determine a student's reading level against a baseline or normed group. Although A, B, and C will be the result of the IRI, D is the most technically correct and the reason for the assessment.
39.	A	2	When discussing behavior in an IEP meeting, it is helpful to have data to support what the teacher is saying. Anecdotal behavior data is qualitative data collected in a causal and informal manner that includes observation notes from the teacher. This is powerful data when looking at behavior and the best option.
40.	B	2	By law, general education teachers must read all of the IEPs of all the students in the class. They must also indicate in their lesson plans how they will accommodate students according to the IEP.
41.	B	2	Because this is a reading assessment, the teacher is not permitted to read the passage for the student. The other 3 accommodations would be permitted as long as they were listed on the student's IEP.
42.	B	2	Testing bias occurs when a group or groups (sex, age, education, race, culture) have an advantage over another. A, C, and D take into consideration bias and make necessary changes or accommodations.
43.	C	2	The key to this question is tracking progress on a weekly basis. The only answer that can do this is curriculum assessments. Curriculum is linked to time because that is how teachers plan instruction throughout the course of the year. A, B, and D do not follow any time component.
44.	C	2	The key term in the question is percentile. This means it was a norm-referenced assessment. B is close, but incorrect because even though it shows a rank of better than 53%, it only accounts for same day and not the normed group. A refers to the percentage score and D only refers to the amount of questions correct and not a score.
45.	C	2	Since the teacher is trying to identify where the student is having issues, she is using formative assessment strategies. If you were unaware of what dynamic assessment was, at least you could pull the word assessment out of it and know that it is the correct answer. A, B, and D are irrelevant to the question.
46.	A	3	Multiculturalism in school is a priority in Florida. B, C, and D all help in creating a culturally diverse classroom.
47.	A	3	It is important to let the question guide you to the answer. Since it states the student has difficulty with a spoon C and D are not correct because those require physical movements. The second part states the difficulty mimicking or copying which is why pictures are out.

#	Answer	Comp	Explanation
			The student's auditory skills were not mentioned which is why process of elimination leads to the correct answer of speaking.
48.	D	3	Anything ever dealing with instructional practices and curriculum have to have some research-based evidence to support it. A, B, and C are factors, but not as important as research.
49.	B	3	Remember anything from a journal or peer-reviewed source counts as research or evidence based which is why B is the correct first choice. A is a good answer, but not the first choice because professional development may not always be around and could be costly. C and D do not have any evidence base behind them.
50.	D	3	The procedural dimension deals with rules and procedures in the classroom that allow it to run efficiently. A deals with teaching style, B deals with the classroom environment, and C deals with how the teacher allows student input.
51.	B	3	The important information in the question is that the student does not like independent learning and is well liked in the classroom by all. Implementing cooperative learning is the best option given the situation. A is not relevant to this question. C is incorrect because you should never reduce curriculum and D deals with reasoning strategies and does not apply.
52.	C	3	Multimodal teaching accommodates all learners through all mediums visually, auditory, and kinesthetically. With various disabilities, A, B, and D will have limitations on learning.
53.	B	3	A task analysis breaks a skill down into manageable components. A deals with a behavior plan, C deals with the goal writing process, and D has to do with a different set of skills.
54.	D	3	The key to this question is that all the subject areas, or curricula, are focusing on one theme throughout the unit. A, B, and C are all types of instruction styles in the classroom.
55.	B	3	Always associate evidence-based instruction with research. A, C, and D reflect opinions and cannot be backed up by reputable research.
56.	C	3	PEMDAS is an example of a mnemonic device. A, B, and D are irrelevant to this question.
57.	A	3	Rubrics are designed to standardize the grading of an assessment. B and D are incorrect because the teacher is not involved in the development. C is incorrect because it defeats the purpose of having a rubric if each student has a different one.
58.	B	3	Technically, the only time a program is allowed to be used in the classroom is if it has research confirming learning results. A is incorrect because the company is biased towards itself. C is incorrect because student's opinions are not the "best information"

#	Answer	Comp	Explanation
			on this decision. D is very important because it deals in funding, but if there is no research on results it doesn't matter.
59.	B	3	Portfolios contain samples of a student's work over a period of time to show growth. B is the only example of the student's own work. A and D should be kept in the student's cumulative file and C is irrelevant to this question.
60.	A	3	Taking turns and sharing fall under social skill behavior. B, C, and D are not relevant to this question.
61.	A	3	Direct instruction is carefully sequenced to provide modeling, guided practice, independent practice and review. B, C, and D do not have the characteristics of sequencing, practice, and repetition.
62.	B	3	Multi-tiered system of supports (MTSS) involves interventions for students who are achieving at different levels. In this case, the word tier is used in the question. Always pay attention to the answer choices in how it relates to the question. The student is receiving tier 3 interventions, therefore B is the best answer.
63.	B	3	Remember, the teacher is there to help the ESE student achieve goals outlined in the IEP. In addition, helping the student do things for herself in the real-world is very important. Therefore, B is the best answer here. All the other answer choices undermine the student's goal.
64.	C	3	*Targeted interventions* is a very good phrase to look for in correct answer choices. The word targeted implies that the interventions will be tailored to the student's needs. Interventions in math decoding is specific for the problem happening with this student. Answer choice C is the best answer here. Never rely solely on the paraprofessional to do the work needed in this situation. Also, never use other students to teach students or to intervene. It's the teacher's job to do this. Bringing it up at the next IEP meeting is not as effective as targeted interventions.
65.	A	3	Flexible grouping is mentioned in the blueprint of the FTCE ESE document. If you see the term flexible grouping in an answer choice, pay attention. Also, flexible grouping is moving students in and out of different groups based on their interests and needs. Static means unchanging, so B is out. Homogenous grouping is grouping all students based on their ability level. Heterogenous grouping is grouping students together with different ability levels.
66.	B	3	Since all the answers are factors and the question asks for the least, it is important to rank them. C would be first because standards supersede everything. A is next because cost and accessibility are important due to budgetary concerns. D would be next because students are important in the process as well as knowing their prior knowledge and how that affects the materials. Therefore, B is the least important factor.

#	Answer	Comp	Explanation
67.	D	3	Differentiated instruction is always a good answer on this exam. Teachers should never simply assign free time to students who are high achievers. They should be challenged. At the same time, those who struggle should receive necessary interventions. D is the best answer here.
68.	A	3	Accommodations during instruction is the best answer choice here. Remember, a teacher should NEVER change the standards or make a lesson easier. What teachers should do is modify instruction or accommodate students to help them achieve. Just using a paraprofessional is not the answer. A paraprofessional should work in tandem with the teacher to help the student.
69.	B	3	When answering this type of question, remember to pick the answer choice that is most appropriate. Reducing the number of problems is better than every other answer. A just adds more time to complete the same overwhelming assignment and C and D is not appropriate for this type of disability.
70.	C	3	A task analysis breaks down certain procedures using charts and visuals. A, B, and D do not apply to this situation.
71.	A	4	The question is asking for two major components. Fidelity means to implement a plan the way it was meant to be designed. B can be part of the checklist but not mandatory, C limits the plan to a certain timeframe, and D excludes peers which can be part of the plan.
72.	B	4	Due to the disability being the factor that led to the incident, the school is under the obligation to provide services to the student. It is important to remember that the setting will change due to the legal issues. A, C, and D are all possible results, except that services must be continued in these places and it is not specified in these answer choices.
73.	B	4	Since the question is asking for data on duration and number of incidents, an observation would be the best selection. A and D are examples associated with the student's learning. C is an already developed scale based on the observations of targeted behavior.
74.	A	4	Although all of the answers are technically anecdotal notes, the question is asking for the best illustration. A provides the most concise, explicit, and detailed information. B, C, and D do not give specifics. A good clue is to go for the answer that contain qualitative data like A.
75.	B	4	The difficulty in this question lies in the subjectivity of the answer choices. All of them are observable, but only a tantrum is measurable. Defined as an emotional outburst associated with emotional distress, a tantrum is a measurable term for a functional behavioral assessment.

#	Answer	Comp	Explanation
76.	C	4	The goal of a functional behavior assessment is to determine the cause of a behavior for the student. A is incorrect because it doesn't involve the student. B would be one of the results of an FBA. D is not the focus of an FBA.
77.	A	4	Anytime there is an incident where a student was restrained, an incident report must be filed. It is required by law that the parents be notified in writing the same day the restraint took place. B is not necessary since administration already processed the student and calmed him/her down. C will occur with the student if a plan is in place, but only after the reports are taken care of and D is not required. A is the only legal requirement of all the answers..
78.	C	4	Planned ignoring is a technique to make a conscious effort to ignore certain behaviors to prevent reinforcing them and is commonly referred to as extinction. A and D are not appropriate because they are negative and refer to consequences. B refocuses the attention of the student and does not apply.
79.	C	4	The purpose of a functional behavior assessment is to continuously monitor interventions to make sure they are properly working. If not, the process starts over again until the behavior is corrected. A, B, and D are not aspects of an FBA.
80.	A	4	In order to understand what environmental factors affect a student's behavior, it is important to conduct observations of the student in the classroom. B, C, and D will not yield accurate enough information as far as environment is concerned.
81.	B	4	A replacement behavior is a behavior you want to use to replace an unwanted target behavior. The target behavior and replacement behavior are both the same and does not address the issue appropriately. C is incorrect because there is no mention of rules and procedures in the question and you cannot assume. A and D are incorrect because they say appropriate.
82.	A	4	Adolescence is a time for students to stand out, fit in, and measure up. B and C are all associated with young elementary aged students. D does not apply to this situation.
83.	A	4	Precorrection is when specific behavioral prompts are used to remind students of the actions they are expected to take to avoid making errors and is also an evidence-based strategy. B and D are incorrect because negative consequences are never the answer. C is not relevant to this situation.
84.	D	4	A token economy rewards good behavior with tokens that can be exchanged for something desired. A, B, and C do not apply to this situation.
85.	D	5	Quadriplegics have no use of their limbs which means they cannot perform tasks involving hands, arms, legs, and/or feet. A and C are

#	Answer	Comp	Explanation
			incorrect because the student cannot touch the screen or type on the desktop. B is incorrect because the student has a speech impairment.
86.	C	5	Expressive language deficit is when a student has difficulty expressing themselves through speech. A is the difficulty in finding the right words for speaking and writing. B is not a deficit and C is when students have trouble making sense of spoken and/or written words.
87.	D	5	Since speaking and hearing are disabled in this student, think of the other senses that can be used such as visual and touch. Communication boards provide visuals to point to in order to communicate non-verbally. A and B are not good choices because the disability limits typing capabilities. C is not good because abbreviations don't teach vocabulary properly.
88.	C	5	Pragmatics is using language in context, especially in conversation. A is the meaning of words, B deals with sounds, and D is all about putting words together.
89.	A	5	Non-verbal is the key term in this question. Picture systems are used with this type of student. The student can present pictures of situations and feelings.
90.	B	5	For unfamiliar subject material, it is always helpful to provide students with background knowledge to help contextualize reading. A, C, and D are good strategies, but the key wording in the question is "unfamiliar topic."
91.	A	5	Processing speed is a contributing factor in learning and attention issues for students with ADHD. B and D have no correlation to ADHD and reading comprehension. C is a reading issue that is independent of ADHD.
92.	A	5	Silent sustained reading should be done on an independent level because it needs little or no instructional support and thus fits this scenario. B is when the teacher provides students with assistance during reading and is not suitable for silent reading. C is when cooperation is encouraged, mostly with other peers. D is a distractor and is not a reading level.
93.	B	5	Language is the most appropriate consideration when dealing with culturally diverse populations. When in doubt match up the answer choices with cultural diversity. A would be right if it stated there was an economically diverse population. C is incorrect because there is no data showing a choice for student interest. D is incorrect because there is no mention of gender.
94.	A	5	The key to this problem is the listening and notetaking skills combined. With a recording the student can focus on listening

#	Answer	Comp	Explanation
			knowing he can take notes after with the recorded audio. B, C, and D are incorrect because they do not address both issues.
95.	D	5	Part of the disproportionality of ELL students in ESE is due to improper assessment. In this case you would want to make sure that the student truly does not know the content and has difficulties leading to placement instead of just not understanding the questions because of the different language. A and B are both reasonable answers, although not the FIRST choice as stated in the question. C has no bearing on placement in a program.
96.	C	5	Collaborative services refer to team teaching. A is when students are taken from the inclusive classroom for services. B is when another teacher checks in with the general education teacher like a supervisor. D means to slowly integrate services as needed with a student.
97.	B	5	The struggling reader will benefit most from echo reading because he is able to hear and see the words and work with the teacher without distraction. A is not a good option because the student may be reading incorrectly and there is no feedback. C is not good enough because working with a peer on grade level may be difficult for the student. D is incorrect because of the age difference and it is not an appropriate strategy.
98.	B	5	Be careful with this question because there are many things going on and most of the answer choices seem right. The key to the question is at the end when the teacher begins to pull back allowing for the student's independence. This is key to scaffolding. A is incorrect because although the teacher does model, there is continued support. C is incorrect because although there is guided practice happening, it doesn't continue for the duration of learning. D is knowledge through experience and not applicable for this scenario.
99.	A	5	Common blends are instrumental when teaching spelling because each letter sound is heard in the word. In this question spelling is the issue of a low-level reader. B, C, and D are valid answers, but the majority of the words, as stated in the question, should come from blends.
100.	C	5	The clue in this question is when it says hear and see, in other words use your senses. A deals with critical thinking skills and B and D are not relevant to this question.
101.	B	5	Error monitoring increases accuracy during independent work without the need for one-on-one instruction. A, C, and D do not address the problem correctly.
102.	A	5	The assistive technology helps the student achieve his or her goals. The technology must be used for the student to be successful and training must be provided to the teacher if she does not know how to use it. Answer choice D is not correct because a teacher cannot

#	Answer	Comp	Explanation
			necessarily be fired immediately for not using the technology. Although, he or she would probably receive a letter of reprimand in his or her file. A is the best answer here.
103.	D	5	Teachers should never make things easier on students. Therefore, A and C are out. Also, teachers should not expect students to work beyond developmental abilities. Activities and lessons should be developmentally appropriate. Teachers should challenge students and offer accommodations and modifications, so students can be successful. This helps to build self-confidence and positive feelings towards learning.
104.	B	5	For students who struggle with listening skills, using explicit and concise directions is key. Also, visual representations of directions will help connect the appropriate behavior to a tangible image.
105.	D	5	Outcome data is all about improvement. Did the students improve in either scores, ability, or behavior? All the other questions are ok. However, they will not yield information on how the students improved. Also, teachers should be concerned about standards; answer D addresses the standards.
106.	A	5	Anytime you see the words relevant or real-world in an answer choice, it is probably the correct answer. Vocab is best taught in context, which means relating it to the real-world.
107.	A	5	Grammar and mechanics are part of the structure of the essay. Syntactic analysis is when the structure of an essay is critiqued by evaluating the student's use of grammar and mechanics.
108.	A	5	Phonemic awareness is the awareness of small sounds in words. Rhyme has to do with the sounds in words.
109.	C	5	Even though this student is writing her name, she is still emerging. She has passed the pre-alphabetic stage if she is using letters to write, but she is not fluent just yet. Automatic is not a writing stage.
110.	B	5	Sight words are words students memorize. They are words like *the, what, why, said, etc*. Students have to simply memorize these words because they appear so frequently in text and general rules may not apply.
111.	D	6	Going to the local store is the key to this question. Community-based instruction provides students real-life experiences out in the community. A and C deal with teaching in the classroom. B deals with teaching students self-reflection, critical thinking, interpersonal skills, etc.
112.	C	6	The teacher is trying to provide a different presentation of the material from the classroom to the real world to allow the students to further understand the concept of the lesson. A is incorrect because accommodations are designed to give equal access to the learning environment and are usually individualized. B is not

#	Answer	Comp	Explanation
			relevant to this question and D means to change what is being taught or expected.
113.	C	6	In Florida, the age of majority is 18 years old.
114.	A	6	ESE students begin to transition to post-secondary planning when they are 16 years old. A transitional IEP replaces the standard IEP during the year in which a student turns 16.
115.	D	6	Life skills are classified as skills needed to operate in the real world as independently as possible. Other life skills include preparing meals, finding transportation (bus, subway, etc.), and knowing how to dial emergency numbers.
116.	B	6	The key is to engage students in real-world application. Therefore, roleplay is the best answer here.
117.	A	6	The students and teachers are planning to ignore the negative behavior because it is part of the student's disability. By including the students, the teacher is helping the students to deal with situations beyond their control.
118.	A	6	To increase positive behaviors and decrease negative behaviors, helping students develop positive self-concepts is key. The best way to do that is to set goals and celebrate gains as students get closer to those goals and eventually meet those goals.
119.	B	6	Strategies for building self-determination skills include having students identify other successful people with disabilities and having students discuss their disabilities with people who can help them. Remember, making lessons easier is NEVER the answer.
120.	C	6	Self-advocacy is the ability to speak and act on behalf of one's self.

This page is left blank intentionally.

Additional ESE Practice

An important skill in slaying the test is the ability to transfer knowledge from one area to another. That way, no matter how the questions are worded, you have the transfer skills and the flexible thinking to answer accurately. We find that writing your own scenarios for each sub-skill on the test is a great way to sharpen your transfer skills. When you write your own scenarios or questions while studying, you're thinking like a test maker and not a test taker!

See the example below.

Write a little scenario or blurb for each subskill. When you can do this, you really know the content.

Competency 1 - Knowledge of the Foundations of Exceptional Student Ed...	
Sub-Skill	**Scenario**
Identify state and federal legislation that govern the education of students with exceptionalities.	
Classify the characteristics of students with exceptionalities using the eligibility criteria of categories included in current state and federal laws and regulations governing K–12 educational programs.	
Compare typical and atypical development of physical, cognitive, linguistic, social, and emotional stages of students in the K–12 educational system.	

The following pages provide an opportunity to write your own test questions for each competency and its sub-skills.

Competency 1 - Knowledge of the Foundations of Exceptional Student Education	
Sub-Skill	**Scenario**
Identify state and federal legislation that govern the education of students with exceptionalities.	
Classify the characteristics of students with exceptionalities using the eligibility criteria of categories included in current state and federal laws and regulations governing K–12 educational programs.	
Compare typical and atypical development of physical, cognitive, linguistic, social, and emotional stages of students in the K–12 educational system.	
Interpret principles and practices in the provision of education for students with exceptionalities based on legal and ethical standards.	
Apply knowledge of the requirements for developing individual educational plans (IEPs), educational plans (EPs), and transition IEPs.	
Evaluate the role and function of systemwide models of support for assisting all students, including students with exceptionalities, in accessing the general education curriculum and achieving high expectations.	
Apply effective methods of communication, consultation, and collaboration with students, parents, caregivers, and all other stakeholders, including those from culturally and linguistically diverse backgrounds, as equal members of educational teams.	
Use effective methods for coaching and supporting paraprofessionals, tutors, and volunteers to assist students with exceptionalities across settings.	
Determine the purposes and functions of professionals, advocacy organizations, and agencies relevant to educating students with exceptionalities.	
Determine the factors associated with disproportionality in exceptional student education	

Competency 2 - Knowledge of Assessment and Evaluation	
Sub-Skill	**Scenario**
Determine the purposes and characteristics of different types of assessments and the appropriate use.	
Apply the legal requirements and ethical principles regarding assessment of students with exceptionalities.	
Identify measurement concepts (e.g., reliability and validity), characteristics, and uses of norm-referenced and criterion-referenced assessments for students with exceptionalities.	
Determine the purpose and requirements for participation of students with disabilities in the statewide assessment program and available accommodations, waivers, and exemptions.	
Interpret and apply the results of formal, informal, and performance-based assessments to address specific needs of students with exceptionalities.	
Analyze assessment data to identify student needs and evaluate student progress in acquiring, generalizing, and maintaining skills across settings.	

Competency 3 - Knowledge of Instructional Practices in Exceptional Student Education	
Sub-Skill	**Scenario**
Select reliable sources of evidence-based instructional practices and interventions.	
Apply appropriate instructional approaches, strategies, and materials based on assessments of the student's educational needs (e.g., grade-level standards, academic and functional performance, effect of exceptionality).	
Choose effective instructional strategies to promote a student's generalization of knowledge and skills across content areas, curriculum, and settings.	
Identify the characteristics and purposes of the core curriculum, supplemental programs, and intensive interventions as they relate to language arts and mathematics in a multi-tiered system of supports.	
Apply techniques for differentiating, accommodating, and modifying classroom instruction to meet the educational needs of individual students with exceptionalities.	
Apply flexible grouping strategies (e.g., academic, behavioral, social) for specific instructional activities.	
Use criteria for selecting and utilizing print and nonprint media for instructional use to match student needs and interests.	
Analyze characteristics of specialized instructional approaches for students with significant disabilities.	

Competency 4 - Knowledge of the Positive Behavioral Support Process	
Sub-Skill	**Scenario**
Identify and choose appropriate prevention and intensive intervention strategies for students who display challenging behaviors.	
Distinguish the various concepts and models of positive behavior support.	
Analyze the legal and ethical issues pertaining to positive behavior support strategies and disciplinary procedures for students with exceptionalities.	
Interpret individual and group data to apply interventions that increase positive behavior.	
Interpret the essential elements of a functional behavior assessment and measure the effects of the behavior intervention plan through data collection strategies.	

Competency 5 - Knowledge of Multiple Literacies and Communication Skills	
Sub-Skill	**Scenario**
Identify language development and the components of language structure.	
Distinguish characteristics of communication disorders and the impact on academic achievement and functional skills.	

Competency 5 - Knowledge of Multiple Literacies and Communication Skills	
Identify appropriate assistive technology and alternative communication systems to facilitate communication across all educational settings.	
Determine the sequence of reading development and the critical components of reading proficiency included in the state standards.	
Apply specialized instructional strategies and techniques to address deficits in phonological processing in students with exceptionalities.	
Apply evidence-based instructional methods for increasing reading proficiency in phonics, word recognition, and fluency that meet the specific educational and functional needs of individual students with exceptionalities.	
Apply evidence-based instructional methods for increasing literacy (e.g., oral language, vocabulary, reading comprehension) in all content areas that meet the specific educational and functional needs of individual students with exceptionalities.	
Determine and apply strategies for facilitating students' critical-thinking, executive functioning, and metacognition skills.	
Select and use effective instructional methods and supports for teaching writing foundations, the writing process, and purposes of writing to meet specific educational and functional needs of individual students with exceptionalities across all content areas.	
Apply evidence-based instructional methods for increasing mathematic skills in all content areas that meet the specific educational and functional needs of individual students with exceptionalities.	

Competency 6 - Knowledge of the Transition Process	
Sub-Skill	**Scenario**
Determine appropriate programs for career development and career and technical education that meet the needs of individual students with disabilities.	
Use results of transition assessments to determine appropriate planning strategies to assist the student, parents, caregivers, and stakeholders in developing postsecondary education, career goals, and postschool outcomes.	
Select instructional approaches to assist students with exceptionalities to engage in self-determination and self-advocacy practices.	
Identify and compare resources and strategies that can assist individual students with disabilities to function independently in postsecondary education, home and community living, and employment.	

This page is left blank intentionally.

Bibliography

American Speech-Language-Hearing Association. (1993). *Definitions of communication disorders and variations* [Relevant Paper]. Available from www.asha.org/policy.

Association for Positive Behavior Support (2018). *What is positive behavior support?* Retrieved from http://www.apbs.org/new_apbs/genintro.aspx#definition

CEEDAR Center (2015). *MTSS for mathematics.* Retrieved from http://ceedar.education.ufl.edu/cems/math/learning-resources/

Center for Parent Information and Resources (2017). Considering LRE in placement decisions. Retrieved from https://www.parentcenterhub.org/placement-lre/

Dill, Margo (2018). Inclusion strategies for mainstreamed classrooms. Retrieved from https://www.brighthubeducation.com/special-ed-inclusion-strategies/71748-using-criterion-referenced-test-results/

Dunlap, G., & Fox, L. (2015). The Pyramid Model: PBS in Early Childhood Programs and its Relation to School-wide PBS. Retrieved from https://www.pyramidmodel.org

Ehri, L. (1999). Phases of development in learning to read words. In J. Oakhill & R. Beard (Eds.), Reading Development and the Teaching of Reading: A Psychological Perspective, 79-108. Oxford, UK: Blackwell Publishers.

Encyclopedia of Mental Disorders (2012). Phonological Disorders. Retrieved from http://www.minddisorders.com/Ob-Ps/Phonological-disorder.html

The Florida Department of Education (2012). *A parent's introduction to exceptional student education in Florida.* Retrieved from http://www.fldoe.org/core/fileparse.php/7674/urlt/0064540-eseparent.pdf

The Florida Department of Education (2018). *Exceptional student education test information guide.* Retrieved from http://www.fl.nesinc.com/PDFs/ESE_TIG_3rdEdition.pdf

The Florida Department of Education (2018). *Secondary transition.* Retrieved from http://www.fldoe.org/academics/exceptional-student-edu/secondary-transition.stml

Florida's MTSS (n.d.). *MTSS implementation components ensuring common language and understanding.* Retrieved from http://florida-rti.org/educatorResources/MTSS_Book_ImplComp_012612.pdf.

Gordillo, W., (2015). Top 10 trends in special education. Retrieved from https://www.scilearn.com/blog/2015-special-education-trends

Harry, B., Klinger, J.K., Sturges, K.M., & Moore, R. (2002). Of rocks and soft places: Using qualitative methods to investigate disproportionality. In D. J. Losen, & G. Orfi eld (Eds.), Racial inequity in special education. Cambridge, MA: Harvard Education Press.

Hurst, S. (2014). What's the difference between RTI and MTSS? Reading Horizons. Retrieved from https://www.readinghorizons.com/blog/what-is-the-difference-between-rti-and-mtss

IDEA Partnership (n.d.) Functional behavior assessment. Retrieved from http://www.ideapartnership.org/documents/ASD-Collection/asd-dg_Brief_FBA.pdf

Madison Metropolitan School District (2014). *Writing instruction and intervention strategies: Initial* guidance. Retrieved from https://mtss.madison.k12.wi.us/files/mtss/Writing_Instruction_and_Strategies.pdf

The National Reading Panel (2016). Five Components of Reading Instruction. Retrieved from http://www.learninglandscape.com/National_Reading_Panel_Reading_Instruction_FAQ.pdf

National Research Council. (2002). Minority students in special and gifted education. Committee on Minority Representation in Special Education, M. Suzanne Donovan and Christopher T. Cross, (Eds.) Division of Behavioral and Social Sciences and Education. Washington, DC: National Academy Press.

Piaget, Jean (1972). The Psychology of Intelligence. Totowa, NJ: Littlefield

Rubin, I. L., & Crocker, A. C. (1989). *Developmental disabilities: Delivery of medical care for children and adults.* Philadelphia: Lea & Febiger.

The Division on Career Development and Transition of the Council for Exceptional Children (2018). *Appendix A: National secondary transition technical assistance center (NSTTAC) age-appropriate transition assessment article.* Retrieved from https://www.iidc.indiana.edu/styles/iidc/defiles/INSTRC/TransitionAssessment/7%20Transition%20Assessment%20Resource%20Guide%20-%20Appendices%20A%20&%20B.pdf

The Florida Department of Education (2017). *Graduation requirements for Florida's statewide assessments*. Retrieved from http://www.fldoe.org/core/fileparse.php/7764/urlt/GradRequireFSA.pdf

The Florida Department of Education (2019). ESE eligibility. Retrieved from http://www.fldoe.org/academics/exceptional-student-edu/ese-eligibility/

The Florida Department of Education (2018). ESE eligibility: Other health impairment (OHI). Retrieved from http://www.fldoe.org/academics/exceptional-student-edu/ese-eligibility/other-health-impairment-ohi.stml.

Florida Professional Development Alternatives (2016). Models of support for inclusive education: Overview. Retrieved from https://fl-pda.org/independent/courses/foundations/pilot/unit2/act2a.htm

The U.S. department of Education (2015). Disabilities discrimination: Overview of the laws. Office for Civil Rights. Retrieved from https://www2.ed.gov/about/offices/list/ocr/disabilityoverview.html

The U.S. Department of Education (2019). Every Student Succeeds Act (ESSA). Retrieved from https://www.ed.gov/essa

The U.S. Department of Education (2019). No Child Left Behind (NCLB). Retrieved from https://www.ed.gov/nclb

Watson, Sue (2018). Practical strategies for special education success in the classroom. Retrieved from https://www.thoughtco.com/practical-strategies-for-the-classroom-3110327

Watson, Sue. (2019). Tips for Working with Students with Severe Handicaps. Retrieved from https://www.thoughtco.com/working-with-students-with-severe-handicaps-3111136

Made in the USA
Columbia, SC
28 January 2020

87211709R00078